Enneagram

The Complete Self-discovery & Self-realization
Through the Wisdom of the Enneagram

(The Enneagram Guide for Change)

John Stover

Published by Knowledge Icons

John Stover

All Rights Reserved

Enneagram: The Complete Self-discovery & Self-realization Through the Wisdom of the Enneagram (The Enneagram Guide for Change)

ISBN 978-1-990084-48-5

All rights reserved. No part of this guide may be reproduced in any form without permission in writing from the publisher except in the case of brief quotations embodied in critical articles or reviews.

Legal & Disclaimer

The information contained in this book is not designed to replace or take the place of any form of medicine or professional medical advice. The information in this book has been provided for educational and entertainment purposes only.

The information contained in this book has been compiled from sources deemed reliable, and it is accurate to the best of the Author's knowledge; however, the Author cannot guarantee its accuracy and validity and cannot be held liable for any errors or omissions. Changes are periodically made to this book. You must consult your doctor or get professional medical advice before using any of the suggested remedies, techniques, or information in this book.

Upon using the information contained in this book, you agree to hold harmless the Author from and against any damages, costs, and expenses, including any legal fees potentially resulting from the application of any of the information provided by this guide. This disclaimer applies to any damages or injury caused by the use and application, whether directly or indirectly, of any advice or information presented, whether for breach of contract, tort, negligence, personal injury, criminal intent, or under any other cause of action.

You agree to accept all risks of using the information presented inside this book. You need to consult a professional medical practitioner in order to ensure you are both able and healthy enough to participate in this program.

Table of Contents

INTRODUCTION 1

CHAPTER 1: THE ROLE OF EMOTIONS AND HOW THOUGHTS AND HABITS AFFECT YOUR EMOTIONS 4

CHAPTER 2: ENNEAGRAM'S BACKSTORY 13

CHAPTER 3: THE REFORMER (TYPE 1) 23

CHAPTER 4: TESTING THE ENNEAGRAM PERSONALITY 43

CHAPTER 5: WHERE ENNEAGRAM WAS DEVELOPED 55

CHAPTER 6: ENNEAGRAM TEST 63

CHAPTER 7: LIFE IS FULL OF CYCLICAL TEMPORAL TRAPS 72

CHAPTER 8: ENNEAGRAM TYPE 1 83

CHAPTER 9: EMOTIONAL INTELLIGENCE 92

CHAPTER 10: THE POWER TO KNOW YOUR TRUE IDENTITY 102

CHAPTER 11: UNDERSTANDING ENNEAGRAM 120

CHAPTER 12: TYPE FOUR - THE ROMANTIC 136

CHAPTER 13: PROTECTING YOURSELF AGAINST UNWANTED EMOTIONS 149

CHAPTER 14: ENNEA-TYPE FIVE – "THE INVESTIGATOR" 161

CHAPTER 15: ENNEAGRAM TYPE 5 - THE OBSERVER 176

CONCLUSION.. 182

Introduction

At its most basic, the Enneagram (pronounced ANY-a-gram) is simply an examination of the nine types of people that exist in the world. Visually, the Enneagram looks like a nine-pointed star within a circle. The word, which is derived from the Greek, literally means "a drawing with nine points." As simple as nine personalities might sound, as you will see throughout this introduction, however, that does not mean that the world can neatly be divided up between the nine types. Instead, the nine types work together in a complex interplay, whereby the adjacent types (wings) can exert influence on a given type. While this influence tends to be fixed, two other points on the circle can influence the given type in different ways, depending on the circumstances in which they find themselves (the security type and the stress type). Together, these different types combine to form a multitude of different personalities. Furthermore, the transformability of any given type means that the Enneagram is not just a diagnostic test, but instead a powerful psychological tool that can help people achieve their ideal sense of harmony and balance by working within their given set of gifts and compensating for their given set of challenges.

This simple yet complicated drawing seeks to provide an explanation as to why each one of us behaves as we do. What is more, it offers to give us guidance about what obstacles might be most perilous for us. Finally, and one of the most important reasons why the Enneagram has achieved such lasting popularity is that it gives specific suggestions as to how we can further our personal development. With the Enneagram, we can strive to improve our relationship to our self, but also to our family, friends, and colleagues. It promises to help us deal with the struggles of life by developing a strategy that works by harnessing our natural strengths and can allow us to work in harmony with our inevitable weaknesses.

Chapter 1: The Role Of Emotions And How Thoughts And Habits Affect Your Emotions

Emotions play a lead role in emotional intelligence. But what are emotions, really? If we are going to be scientific about it, emotions are neural impulses that propel an organism to act as a response to stimuli, both physical and perceived, in its overall need to cope or survive. In other (perhaps simpler) words, emotions are feelings that are expressed through physiological functions such as facial expressions, heart rate, crying, aggressiveness, or self-preservation.

Human emotions are differentiated from the rest of the animal kingdom in that they are pleasant or unpleasant mental states interpreted in the mammalian brain's limbic system. These emotional states are manifested through non-verbal expressions of love, agreement, anger, fear, dislike, sadness, shame, etc. Take love, for instance: it's been theorized as a feeling designed for caring, feeding, and grooming of offsprings originating from a nerve cell network in the brain.

Emotions can be fleeting, such as a flare of irritation with a co-worker, or they can be lingering, such as an enduring sadness from a loss of a loved one. Generally, we can all agree that emotions play a very important role in our thoughts and actions. Our emotions compel us to act in certain ways and influence our decisions greatly.

Emotions are important as they motivate us to take action or make decisions that we hope will bear the best possible impact. Feelings of anxiety over, say an impending exam, pushes us to prepare, study, or rehearse. Likewise, humans are somehow wired to seek social activities or hobbies that will bring forth positive feelings of fulfillment and avoid situations that are potentially boring, stressful, or dangerous.

Emotional health

Getting a better grip of one's emotions is like a series of exercises towards the road to emotional health. People who are said to be "emotionally healthy" are easy to identify: they are individuals who are characteristically aware of their thoughts, feelings, and behaviors. These people have naturally integrated healthy ways to cope with difficulties into their very lifestyles. Problems or stress of any form seem to faze them in no considerable way. Emotionally healthy people generally exude a self-aware and confident air about them and they are highly capable of maintaining positive relationships.

Being emotionally healthy does not mean that you are totally worry-free and are "happy all the time". Having good emotional health means you have a solid grasp of your emotions – you are able to deal with your feelings, whether positive or negative. It is but natural to still have feelings of sadness, anger, stress, and frustration. What distinguishes emotionally healthy people from the rest is that they are able to manage negative feelings of this kind. They can easily tell when a difficulty is more than they are able to handle on their own. Emotionally healthy people do not shirk seeking help, whether professionally or from their trusted support systems.

Our thoughts, then, figure significantly in staying emotionally healthy. Being constantly conscious about your thought processes will greatly impact the train of emotions to actions. Speaking in fitness terms, an honest awareness of your own emotions and how you react make for great "warm-up". Recognize and acknowledge those things in your life that frustrate you, sadden you, and anger you. Address those things by changing them, accepting them, or avoiding them altogether. Not exactly talking about escapism here, but you do not need to seek out the drama, so to speak. Or, in simpler terms: pick your battles. This allows you the ability to express your emotions appropriately. Allow yourself time to think and calm down before doing or saying things you might later regret.

Mayer and Geher, in their study on Emotional Intelligence and the Identification of Emotion, wrote that "people who are good at connecting thoughts to feelings may better 'hear' the emotional implications of their own thoughts, as well as understand the feelings of others from what they say."[1]

With this said, we should all strive to keep our thoughts under control. We might not have total control of the emotion we feel at any given moment. But, by staying focused on our thoughts, we can control our reaction to those emotions. As the saying goes: "You cannot prevent a bird from landing on your head. But you can keep it from building a nest."

So, okay, maintaining an objective view of your thoughts as much as possible is crucial in how you interact with everyone else on a daily basis. But how do you make sure your thoughts, as with your emotions, are healthy?

You can stay on top of your thought processes by managing your stress. As much as it is possible, try to change those situations that are typical sources of stress for you. You, of course, will not be able to change everything… so it is ideal if you also strive to learn relaxation techniques that will help you cope. Deep breathing, meditation, exercise, pursuing a talent… there are countless ways to help keep yourself grounded and level-headed in the face of stressors. Find the "sweet spot" between work and play, occupation and rest. Leave time for your hobbies or passions. This healthy balance will help you stay focused on the positive things in your life. You might agree that the beauty of life lies in its imperfections, its unpredictability. Disappointment is inevitable – know how to forgive yourself and others for mistakes. Share this positivity, too, by establishing and harnessing reliable relationships with other people. Humans are social creatures, by nature, and positive connections substantially contribute to one's holistic well-being. Make time for lunch dates and catch-ups; join groups; greet strangers.

Finally – and I can never be more willing to overwork a known cliché right now – take care of your health. Your mental health is hitched on the state of your physical well-being. A mediation analysis was conducted about the relationship between physical and mental health looking at data around direct and indirect effects of past mental health on present physical health and past physical health on present mental health using lifestyle choices and social capital.

We find significant direct and indirect effects for both forms of health, with indirect effects explaining 10% of the effect of past mental health on physical health and 8% of the effect of past physical health on mental health. Physical activity is the largest contributor to the indirect effects. There are stronger indirect effects for males in mental health (9.9%) and for older age groups in mental health (13.6%) and in physical health (12.6%).[2]

Exercise regularly, eat healthy, and get enough sleep. Do not underestimate the desirable effects of exercise on clarity of the mind. You might have heard about endorphins – hormones secreted by the brain after physical exertion. These neurochemicals interact with the receptors in your brain and reduce the perception of pain. Endorphins also set off a positive feeling in the body, similar to the effects of morphine. But do not abuse substances like drugs or alcohol. These mostly synthetic substances have addictive qualities that inflict harmful effects on the body (not to mention, the mind) with prolonged or excessive use.

Sustain your mind and body with healthy habits. Filling your day-to-day existence with positively-impacting habits will greatly enhance how you perceive situations, conceive your thoughts, understand how you feel, and ultimately, how you express your reactions.

Chapter 2: Enneagram's Backstory

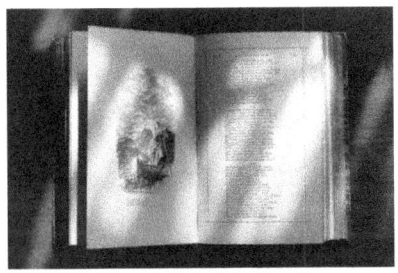

Where exactly the beginning of our modern version of the enneagram model was first accepted is often a subject of debate between those who specialize in the enneagram and other personality models like it. However, many people agree that the place where the first version of the enneagram began was in the writings of a 4th century mystic named Evagrius Ponticus, who posited that there were 8 specific "deadly thoughts" which could be used to categorize sinful people under, with an overarching concept of self-love which had power over these eight deadly thoughts. The term of "enneagram" itself is commonly accredited to G.I Gurdjieff, who founded the fourth way enneagram, not the enneagram that is used in its place today. That model of enneagram, with the wings, center, the nine basic types, was mainly brought into existence by Oscar Ichazo.

While the enneagram has gone through more than its fair share of different tellings and iterations, today we land on the form of enneagram which is used to determine which of 9 basic types a person falls under, along with other details of the personality type which surround those nine basic categories. This contemporary enneagram model is visually represented by a 3-part shape—an outer circle, an inner triangle, and an irregular hexagon. In more spiritual interpretations of the visual of the enneagram, the circle around all nine of the basic types signifies unity of the types, while the inner triangle and hexagon represent the laws of three and seven respectively.

While the structure is sound both in theory and visually, the enneagram should not be used as a foundation for the way to conduct yourself. The enneagram test and your results should however, serve as a kind of cornerstone in your path to self-discovery. When you learn more about yourself, the enneagram may play a rather large role in that path. It may offer you a lot of crucial information and advice about yourself and your relationships, as well as very sound advice into a predicament you may be experiencing because of your enneagram type. However, the enneagram test is not something that can be empathetic, or tailored specifically to you as an individual or to your dilemma. It's best to take the word of the enneagram test to heart, but not to rely on it for every problem that you face. Instead, consult with those who are also on their self-discovery journey, perhaps others who have found themselves in the enneagram test. These people that you meet, regardless of how much they know about you or relate to you, will be able to help you more on a certain problem than a test which cannot understand you on any level other than your enneagram type.

The test is one to be used as a guideline for certain behaviors that you might find bothersome to yourself or to others. If you find yourself indulging in a behavior that is negative or which you would like to control but can't seem to shackle down, it may correspond to your type. Therefore, the advice that your enneagram results give you are best used as a broad tool for self-improvement, not as a tool to base your life around. Instead, tailor your results to mean something within the context of your life, instead of the other way around.

You may be able to predict your enneagram type before you take the definitive test, if you learn more about the types and how they correspond to behavioral tendencies. If you find that you happen to be incredibly centered around cooperation in a group, and are always the one in a group project who deescalates tensions and always tries to find a way which will benefit the harmony of the group, you may predict that you're the ninth type, the peacemaker, before you even take the test. Of course, depending on your answers on the test, you may receive a completely different answer from the exam than what you had thought of yourself, but at least you had an idea of one of your outstanding traits. Whether or not you would then decide to act upon that character trait to better yourself is then entirely up to you. Someone who finds themselves much more reserved than the rest of their family or friend group may think of themselves as being the individualist type, but may be an entirely different type after receiving legitimate results.

As many combinations as there can be of different components within the enneagram, there can never be enough to totally encompass the potential combinations of traits within a person which you otherwise crash. There are some people who are both generous and selfish at times, who are both kind-hearted but appear cold. These seemingly contradictory traits can alter the results of a personality test, and the mindset you're in when you take the enneagram can affect your results. However, answering honestly may allow for the enneagram to pick up on this contradiction, and incorporate it into the results for that individual in particular.

Additionally, there are people who want to act a certain way but may have other factors which don't allow them to do so, or don't allow them to as much as they would like. Experiencing trauma can affect a person so much as to alter their personality, to the point where who they "used to be" may be entirely separate from their demeanor post a traumatic incident. This can skew the result of any personality test, enneagram included, because the temporary demeanor of a person who has just undergone something traumatic or life-changing may act differently than they would have years ago, or will act again years later. It can make a person feel as though their self after a traumatic incident is broken, or not right compared to their former demeanor. So, it's not recommended that the enneagram test be taken by someone who has recently undergone something which would allow for imperfect or plainly inaccurate test results.

As always, part of the quest into understanding the enneagram also becomes a quest into the human condition, and motivation behind decisions. Why are we motivated the way that we are, and how do we define sentience? While these questions are enigmatic in themselves, they can be summarized in a more concise manner—why do we do what we do?

The answer to this question is different for many people. Some people define their motivation for many of their life choices as feeling duty-bound—some feel they are simply fulfilling their destiny. Others do what they do out of a more hedonistic outlook—do what you want, when you want. Many people have different outlooks on their motivation for their behavior, but what part of that personality is actually built into them, and what part of that is totally devoted to the people they've grown up around?

As it turns out, that answer depends on what aspect of the personality you're addressing in particular. Studies find that of the 5 main aspects of personality—openness, conscientiousness, extraversion, agreeableness, and neuroticism—vary in how inheritable they are. While being open to new topics, being imaginary, and being creative are the most inherited from your parents, how laid back or easy-going you are is the most dependent on your environment and experiences. But, if you round them all out, all of the main personality traits are about half inherited, half learned. That leaves for, in many cases, over half of your personality to be derived from what you do in your life, where you live, who you make friends with, your work environment, etc. So, the enneagram, and all personality tests, are not just machines that tell you that you're actually growing up to be the next version of your father.

More of your personality than not is, to an extent, your choice.

While we may often feel out of control of where our lives are headed, or out of control of our own behavior, examinations like the enneagram are ones that show us that we truly have the most power over ourselves and our behavior than anyone else in the world. Throughout the course of this venture into the enneagram structure and the personality test, the power of choice becomes more and more important throughout, just as it becomes more and more important as we navigate our way through our own lives.

Chapter 3: The Reformer (Type 1)

Also known as the Perfectionist

Fifteen Signs You're a Reformer

You strive to make the world a better place in which to live. You are capable of seeing, in clear detail, what is wrong with a situation and you are prepared to take the necessary steps to rectify matters.

You possess a very strong sense that you have a life purpose or a mission to fulfill.

Other people often describe you as being responsible, dependable and brimming over with common sense. They can also sometimes accuse you of having no feelings. (You **do** have feelings – you're just keeping them all in!)

You think you have to do everything perfectly, going so far as to think that **you** yourself have to be perfect.

You are highly self-disciplined - sometimes to a fault. You have little to no trouble sticking to a schedule or routine.

You hate feeling stagnant and you always ache to be useful in some way.

You feel you have to keep a lid on all your very strong wants and needs.

It is vitally important to you that you 'do the right thing.'

You have an intense fear of making mistakes or blunders.

You tend to experience tension in your shoulders, neck and jaw.

It sometimes takes you longer than the average person to complete a task, which is, of course, because of your exceptional eye for detail.

You can be very critical of yourself and others.

You may experience disappointment and frustration at those times when reality does not meet your expectations.

You hold yourself to very high standards of excellence.

Does this sound anything like you?

The Reformer: An Overview

Perfectionism can be a double-edged sword. On the one hand, it can cause impressive and wonderfully satisfying results. On the other, it can lead to wounding self-criticism and even inaction, where the perfectionist might not even begin a task for fear of failure.

Type One in The Enneagram model is not lacking in the least when it comes to admirable traits such as reliability, honesty, common sense, integrity and nobility. In fact, this type can be downright heroic. They could, however, learn to be kinder to themselves. Although lowering your standards is not usually to be recommended, Ones could sometimes benefit from taking such advice, as the expectations they heap upon themselves - and others - can be unrealistically and punishingly high.

This type wishes to make the world a better place, and what's not to like about that?! High ideals are the order of the day, coupled with a strong sense of purpose.

These people get things done and done right!

You might also recognize a One by their fastidious attention to detail: that go-to co-worker who you can always rely on. Granted, they may take longer than most to complete the task, but the end result will be undoubtedly flawless. Or it might be the friend with the incredible self-discipline, who will keep to the diet or the exercise regime and whose gym membership will be used beyond the third week in January.

If you want to keep in a One's good books, make sure you keep your promises. **Never** say you are going to do something and then back out or forget about it. This is a complete no-no and breaks their ethical code. These good people would never do the same to you! And don't forget to take things seriously. This type does not appreciate a flippant attitude. It will surprise and delight them if you join them in speculating about how things can be improved in the world, and you will make all their dreams come true by actually taking action. Encourage them also to be less critical of themselves. Teach them that a little self-kindness goes a long way. Above all, a One needs a friend who can coax them to have fun and to take life - and themselves - a little less seriously.

The Reformer Levels

Healthy

Heroism

Type Ones on The Enneagram are the stuff that heroes are made of. A man by the name of Gandhi comes to mind. He embodied the qualities of the One at his or her best, in his capacity for extraordinary wisdom and discernment. His humanity inspired immense loyalty and made him a great leader that thousands of people felt compelled to follow. And we need look no further than Joan of Arc for a historical example of a One who uplifted many and created change through the courage of her conviction and willingness to self sacrifice.

Not every One can be a Gandhi or a Joan of Arc, but within their own private sphere of influence, no matter how big or small, they can often perform acts of everyday heroism.

Practical Action

It is one thing to have lofty ideals. It is quite another to act in accordance with them. But the One is a master of practical action, striving always to be useful, to fix the things that they consider broken and to fulfil their powerful mission in life. These people put their money where their mouth is. They have no qualms around making personal sacrifices to serve a higher cause.

Loyalty

The Reformer will not say one thing and then do another. They are impeccable with their word. Neither will they make promises to do something and then not do it. If you are lucky enough to have the friendship of a One, you know that you have someone who will always have your back.

Attention to Detail

A One will not leave a job half-done. Neither will they turn in a shoddy project. They always strive for excellence, in thought, word and deed. This type is always pushing the envelope and raising standards - for themselves and the world in which they live. Consider these prominent Ones in the areas of politics, business and entertainment. Such people as: Nelson Mandela, Michelle Obama, Anita Roddick (The Body Shop), Martha Stewart, Dame Maggie Smith and Meryl Streep, Confucious, Margaret Thatcher, Plato, George Bernard Shaw, Noam Chomsky, Emma Thompson, Jane Fonda, Jerry Seinfeld, George Harrison, Hilary Clinton, Jimmy Carter, Prince Charles.

Integrity

A One's deep sense of integrity makes him or her an excellent teacher and, in general, a witness and proponent of the truth.

They are principled to the core and will uphold these principles even at the cost of their own safety or comfort. You can trust them to always do the right thing, even if this goes against conventional wisdom or public opinion. The Reformer will not be swayed from what he or she believes to be right and good.

Neutral or Average

Dissatisfaction

The Reformer at this level thinks it is up to them to fix everything. They feel they know how everything 'should' be done and that it is their absolute duty to tell everybody else what they should do too!

Rigidity

This rigidity is caused by the fear of making a mistake. Everything has to be exactly right. There is no margin for error whatsoever, either for the Reformer themselves or for those around them.

Overly critical

The Reformer directs this criticism - not just at him or herself - but at others too.

They feel the need to correct people constantly, and not in an especially sensitive way! Very low level of satisfaction.

Unhealthy

Hell is other people!

It's not always easy being a Reformer. You will constantly encounter those with different value systems to your own and this might well upset your high-minded ideals and insistence on excellence. It may lead you to be self-righteous, intolerant, dogmatic or inflexible. You might severely judge others for their inability to see things in the same way that you do.

Obsession

There is a risk that Ones can become obsessive in nature. This can manifest itself in a number of ways. One of these is in the area of diet and nutrition. In extreme cases, the Reformer's quest for self-control might lead to conditions such as anorexia and bulimia. Some might also resort to alcohol in order to alleviate the stress that they put themselves under. Obsessive Compulsive Disorder is also a danger to this type.

Anger

The Reformer can get angry very easily and this anger can often have a tinge of self-righteousness to it. Offense may be taken easily, from other people's refusal to do what the One believes to be right. This anger - however righteous - can unfortunately have the effect of alienating others. This is a great pity, as Ones often have a very valid point to make. Repressing this anger is not the answer either, as this might manifest in health issues such as high blood pressure or ulcers.

Depression

This is a fate that can befall a person with a dominant Type One personality, when the trait takes an unhealthy turn. A less than healthy Reformer can be extremely condemnatory, not to mention cruel, to themselves and others. Depressions, breakdowns and suicide attempts are the worst possible outcome here.

Unrealistically High Standards

Enneagram Type Ones can struggle with intense disappointment when reality does not match up to their expectations. It can make them appear overly negative or critical of other family members, friends or co-workers. It can make them very harsh task masters - pedantic and unforgiving. It is not pleasant to be on the receiving end of an unhealthy One's constant criticism and disappointment at your efforts.

But it's not all doom and gloom!

So, if you are a One - a Perfectionist, a Reformer - how can you best avoid the potential pitfalls and instead bring out the best in what your personality type has to offer?

The Reformer Wings

Type One with a Two wing (1W2)

What do you get when you cross a Type One with a Type Two? Well, for a start, the One becomes less repressed and a little more emotionally balanced by the two's directedness and desire to please others.

This is often a very neat and tidy-looking person. The One gives them a propensity for perfectionism and the Two makes them more sensitive to criticism. In other words, they don't want to be criticized about their appearance. So their hair will be perfect and clothing will be just so. They might hold themselves very correctly and come across as having rather a condescending attitude.

This subtype is very hard on his or herself. They will make every effort to do the right thing and if they can also manage to please others in the process, that's even more preferable.

The healthy version of a One with a Two wing is a more relaxed version of a full One with less of an inclination to be righteously judgmental. They can actually believe and admit that they might not always be right!

The One enjoys correcting others. With the influence of the Two, the corrections become more helpful and less intrusive. They are also better able to tolerate differences with the benefit of the Two wing.

If the Reformer with the Two wing happens to experience a kind of spiritual awakening, he or she can become a most inspiring teacher who can bring joy and compassion to their practice. One is wise and Two is loving. At their best, this sub type can be a sterling friend who always seems to know the right thing to say or do.

But oh dear! Things can take a turn for the worse when the Reformer's not so emotionally healthy and mature. The One's perfectionism combined with the Two's pride can lead to trouble. It can amount to great inner conflict. Self-critical introspection goes into overdrive and may be accompanied by fits of rage which descend into self-judgement and remorse.

When severely unhealthy, the anger and pride combine to create despair. Here, the One with a Two wing will punish themselves endlessly and suicide might even be the end result.

It is not surprising the Reformer with a Two wing might enjoy work that involves helping other people become perfect. Examples of such would be teachers, dieticians and judges.

Type One with a Nine wing (1W9)

The combination of the perfectionism and judgement of Type One with the withdrawal from stress of Type Nine makes for a quiet, conservative and somewhat repressed sub type. They do not show a lot of emotion and they will come across as quite strict, quiet and practical. They are slow to express their views also but will usually act from principled judgement.

They can, of course, shine when emotionally healthy and mature. Here, they will learn to access an inner warmth and be capable of bringing it to the fore. Although they might still be a little judgmental, they allow for the fact that they are capable of getting it wrong at times. And anyway, it doesn't really matter that much after all. They learn at this stage to control the propensity of the Nine to withdraw under stress and this allows them to participate in life more fully. They are gentle, responsible, fun-loving and capable of relaxing and just letting go.

At their very best, they will be ever more joyful and participate in life with much gusto. They will have high self-esteem at this level. The wisdom of the One will merge with the selflessness of the Nine and can allow them to obtain significant spiritual advancement.

But this sub type can be unhealthy too and when they are, they might try to exert too much control over their emotions which will lend to them a physical rigidity punctuated by fissions of explosive energy.

Repressed emotions are ever present under the surface and they will come across as "nervy" types. They will be hostile and withdrawn and suffer from self-hatred. They might be highly suspicious and engage in passive-aggressive behaviour. Most of this will be bottled up.

If things disintegrate even further, they can come across as robotic and ritualistic. Anxiety about performing routines just right can become extreme. They may descend into psychosis and become paralyzed with inaction.

This variant of the One stands upright and offers few, but genuine, smiles. It is possible that they are drawn to work that expresses their talent for performing precise tasks, such as accountancy or computer programming.

Advice For The Reformer

I know you didn't ask for advice, but we're going to give it to you anyway! As a Reformer, you probably don't feel you need any counsel, because of your higher than average sense of right and wrong and your intense feeling of purpose. And you are right, to a point. We each need to follow our own star. However, we all have our weaknesses too, and it can be very useful at times to have a second eye, as it were, to give us a greater sense of perspective.

Keep in mind that not everyone will see the world in such black and white terms as you do. There are numerous shades of grey and sometimes you need to make allowances for middle-ground.

Find a healthy way to express and release your anger, one that doesn't involve another human having to feel the full extent of your wrath but at the same time, means you don't repress it all, which could lead to serious health problems for you. It may also help to find less reasons to be angry. Accepting other people's imperfections, perhaps! Don't forget that people can be chaotic. If someone turns up late for an appointment, it doesn't necessarily mean that they disrespect you or don't value your time. They might just be struggling with the messiness of their own lives. Be less critical of others. And while you're at it, be less critical of yourself too!

Keep in mind the famous serenity prayer: Grant me the serenity to accept the things I cannot change, the courage to change the things I can and the wisdom to know the difference.

Be cognizant that you have a tendency to store tension in your body, particularly in your jawline, neck and shoulders. Consider taking steps to counteract this, such as meditation, massage or other relaxation techniques. And why not try to have fun! This is a proven and excellent path to relaxation. After all, nobody likes a martyr!

It is possible that you had parents with very high expectations of you. If this is the case, perhaps it is now time to re-parent yourself and show yourself more softness and kindness. Remember: 'Angels fly because they take themselves lightly.' You don't have to take yourself so seriously all the time. And remind yourself often that everyone makes mistakes, including you. You are not a failure if you make a mistake. This is how we learn. Acceptance of this is key. Furthermore, it is perfectly acceptable to have human emotions and impulses. And sometimes 'good enough' is good enough. Perfection is an illusion. So forgive yourself for your imperfections. Forgiveness is a gift to yourself even more so than to the one that you are forgiving.

You often feel that the weight of the world is on your shoulders. Thankfully, it is not. You are just one person and you are doing just fine.

Trust your inner guidance and most of all, trust life.. Your tendency to see so clearly where things need to be improved, can make you blind to the many things that are right with the world. If you look more closely, you will recognize that things are often working out.

Try not to be too disappointed or impatient if those around you don't change immediately in accordance with what you might have taught them. It does not mean that you are not a gifted teacher, but rather that everyone develops at their own pace. Patience is a virtue!

Above all, don't stop being who you are. There is a reason you were born this way so find out why and make the most of it!

Chapter 4: Testing The Enneagram Personality

The personality types that have been discussed thus far are largely determined by the answering of several questions that are meant to judge various aspects of the personality in order to create an accurate assessment. There are several different tests available to you online, both free and paid. They are largely related to each other. If you do not wish to pay for a test, you could try taking two or three free assessments in order to ensure that the types are the same to determine your own type. This chapter will primarily discuss what the Enneagram test is looking for, as well as how it works to create the end results. Lastly, it will end with several sample questions. Because these tests are quite intensive and involve a massive amount of scoring, one will not be provided for you within this book. Please feel free to look for one online before continuing in order to get the most out of your reading of this book!

Enneagram Tests

This test can be directly compared to the Big Five and Myers-Briggs personality tests, providing yet another aspect that an individual can use in order to really understand who they are as an individual. This particular test is far more focused on the individual's personality type while also giving consideration to how it interacts with others as well.

Enneagram tests are entirely based on the individual's own self-reporting, making some people dubious about how well it actually describes someone's personality type. After all, look at several different personality disorders—narcissists believe that they are the most perfect, worthy of admiration people there could be, while those with BPD may believe that they are inherently flawed beyond repair, and that is why they believe they are constantly abandoned. How we view our own personality types can be particularly inaccurate in these situations—it is entirely possible that someone reports their ideal personality type rather than who they actually are.

Nevertheless, it is an important tool to use. Most of the time, you will find yourself given several traits in contrasting pairs while you are told to rate where you believe you fall on that spectrum. When you do this, you are rating your own quotient of that particular trait, which is then cross-checked with the traits of the Enneagram types.

When you take an Enneagram test, it is important to make your answers as accurate as possible. Make sure that you are always honest with yourself as you answer these questions to get an accurate response. If you do not know where to place yourself on a scale or how to answer a question, always go with your gut reaction, and if you do not even have a gut reaction, try to consider who you were as a young adult, before life experience may have taught you to suppress certain tendencies or habits.

How It Works

These tests will ask you several questions, likely more than 100, and then score you accordingly. They will usually take you between 10 and 20 minutes, depending on your own speed when it comes to reading and answering. Once you have answered all of the questions, they will be scored accordingly in order to identify how closely you relate to each of the personality types. The type that you are the most closely related to will be your dominant type.

Of course, for some people, they may get an answer that they did not expect, or that they did not like. You may have favored yourself as an Observer but found out that actually, you were a Perfectionist all along. When this happens, keep in mind that you have decided to take a test to get the most accurate results. You will need to keep an open mind and realize that, despite the fact that we believe that we know ourselves intimately, more than anyone else possibly would, it is entirely possible that you have misinterpreted your own beliefs toward yourself.

If you have remained honest with your test in identifying your personality, the chances are that your results are accurate, whether you like them or not. Instead of getting upset or annoyed over results, instead, think of the benefits that you have gathered simply through learning the truth. You will be able to see what your biggest weaknesses are thanks to the fact that you now know the truth. You will see what your strengths are as well, and in learning these strengths and weaknesses, you can start to better your relationships.

Criticisms of the Enneagram

Of course, as already touched upon, it is hard to get solid evidence and results when a test is subjective. After all, what one person may see as perfectionistic, another may see as something entirely different. You may feel like you are a shy person, despite the fact that you are adept at dealing with other people. This could run into discrepancies in which someone may score themselves to be a Type 1 person while someone else with similar personality features but a differing viewpoint may get an entirely different result altogether.

Other People

Another common criticism of the Enneagram is the fact that people believe that it is entirely based on pseudoscience—they say there is no possible way that a handful of questions can reduce someone down into a personality type that will have the exact same tendencies as someone else with that same personality type. However, keep in mind that this tool is not meant to be scientific. It is not meant to define people to diagnose them, but rather is an important tool for self-reflection and insight into who you are as an individual. It is not being used therapeutically, and instead, since it is able to be quite informative for someone who may not really know who they are without some help, it should be left alone. Despite the lack of peer-reviewed studies, it is just as valid and important thanks to the insight that people gain.

Lastly, it is believed that the personality types are just as vague as horoscopes— they fall into what is known as the Barnum Effect, in which something is just vague enough to be relatable, which allows people to see meaning where there really is none in the first place. This is the same principle that scammers trying to get people to believe in their fortune-telling abilities use—they say things that are just vague enough to allow for it to hold true in a variety of situations, and people latch on to that to give meaning.

Keep in mind that this is not a diagnostic criteria. It is designed to allow for personal insight rather than for use in any sort of psychological processes. When you treat this as a personal self-discovery tool, you will find it to be a valuable resource.

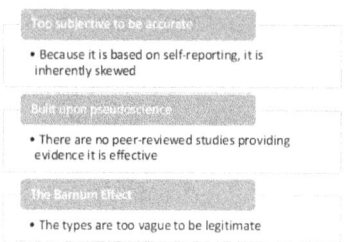

Sample Questions

Now at this point, we will go over some sample questions that you may see on an Enneagram test. Feel free to answer these yourself as you go through them. As you do, see if you can start to piece together your own Enneagram type, or perhaps, it will provide you with the insight you need later as you read about each type to determine which is the most accurate for you.

Indicate whether you think the following statement is accurate or inaccurate for you on a scale of 1-5. Let 1 be not accurate at all, 3 be neutral, and 5 be accurate.

I try my best to be helpful

I must be accomplished what I set out to do without failure

I want other people to like me

I feel a wide range of emotions

I am a deep or philosophical thinker

I feel like I do not truly belong anywhere

I am always prepared, no matter what happens

I can always find something positive, no matter how bad the situation

I domineer over decision-making

I often get lost in daydreams

Select which statement is more accurate for you:

I place more value on:

Getting things done on time as promised

Having a good time, even at the cost of not completing work

I see the future as:

Exciting and positive

Concerning and negative

I always try to ensure that:

Everyone is on task

Everyone has had their needs met

I typically:

Dwell on the past, particularly when it has been hurtful

Push past the pain and move on

I want to be seen as:

Successful and accomplished, having achieved my goals

Unique and memorable

I want to:

Stand out amongst a crowd

Blend in within the crowd

I value most:

My relationships

My work and success

When angry, I:

Struggle to express that anger to others

Have no issues expressing my anger

I focus more on:

My feelings over the feelings of other people

Other people's feelings over my own

People commend me for my:

Knowledge and intelligence

My toughness or tenacity

Answer true or false to the following statements:

I am rarely or never depressed, or I do not get depressed easily

I am too strict

I typically trust people, even when I do not know them well or at all

I find great joy in taking care of other people—I really excel at it

I desire success and recognition at all costs—they are the most important end-goals

I need to win at a game or sport in order to feel like I am really enjoying it

I typically give more than I take when in close interpersonal or romantic relationships

It is difficult for me to stay on task and get my work done, especially when there is something that I would rather do instead.

My workplace and home are often quite neat and tidy—I value keeping everything organized

I am romantic at heart and will show it in relationships

Of course, the tests that you will encounter online will often involve far more than just a handful of questions— you will often see several dozen, or even upwards of 200 sometimes in order to get a clear idea of where you belong on the scale. When you have nine different traits that you are testing for, of course, you will need several dozen questions in order to get an accurate idea of how closely you can relate to any specific Enneagram type.

Chapter 5: Where Enneagram Was Developed

The exact nature of where Enneagram originated has been a mirage since its inception in the 4th century. As noted from the beginning of this book, contextual understanding of Enneagram has been developed through various conceptions and teachings from scholars with diverse ideas. Many people who published works to influence others on the nature of Enneagram never had the intention of the deduced meanings. Interestingly, one of the concepts of psychology that have suffered a lot of false conceptions is Enneagram.

Many people that start Enneagram do so with what could be considered diluted knowledge regarding where it was initially developed. Different conceptions of Enneagram have contributed immensely to what we know it as today. Here, the 'places' where Enneagram was developed are the most prominent ones throughout its history. They are where Enneagram can best be understood and found. They are the teachings of the notable more profound of the Enneagram personalities.

Since Enneagram has entertained different approaches and alarming concern from different professions –such as psychology, neurology, theology, and lots more –the need to understand where it was developed rose to some degree. It is pertinent to note that where Enneagram of personality developed from, as discussed here, is based on the diverse scholars of the Enneagram and not that there is a concrete building like a pyramid of Egypt or a monument center that begat it.

Additionally, Enneagrams development is based on the fact that there are different schools of thoughts with different terminologies. As well as approaches, conception, overlapping and merging, teachings, dealings, etc. The Enneagram we have today, though quite different from its original intention, is gotten from the places it evolved.

In past studies, psychologists have identified six basic 'places' where Enneagram originated. Keep in mind that this is different from the history of the Enneagram. The origins and places where it was developed to simplify the teachings of the developers. Below are the six 'places' where Enneagram was developed:

Don Richard Riso

Don Richard Riso is a neurotic approach to the study of the Enneagram. Its manner of dealing is to give a full description of the sequence in the nine personalities from the neurotic approach through to normal development and then to healthy emotion. The development of this kind of Enneagram was based on giving an analysis of how emotional health has evolved using the neurons in the body. Based on this approach and development, there have been many beliefs and teachings on this kind of Enneagram personality. It contributes to where the enneagram personality was developed.

Oscar Ichazo development of enneagram personalities

An approach that is based on Ichazo was developed in order to give the application of the nine personalities using varying schemata like ego and fixations in order to provide an analysis of self-development. Many books have used this approach where enneagram personalities had been developed both in the application and in actual teachings. The goal of the Enneagram in this approach is to provide the schema in self-development using the fixations theories.

Hameed A. Ali (A. S. Almaas) development of Enneagram personalities

Hameed A. Ali's development of Enneagram personalities is a psychological approach which evolved as another different kind of Enneagram. With this approach, Enneagram of personality is only a combination of studies from disciplines in the therapy of Gestalt through to that of Zen and the Reichian. It is purely psychological, thus studies the mind as well as how they affect human behavior. This particular type of Enneagram is probably the type that had received the most publications and teachings. This is likely due to the fact that it is one of the most fundamental things to humans –the mind. This has been considered as one of the comprehensive approaches to ascertain where the Enneagram of personalities has developed.

Claudio Naranjo development of enneagram personalities

Being a psychiatrist, Claudio proposed an approach that substitutes and replaces the usage of neurotic terms and strategies with psychiatric jargons and dealings. The total reliance on neurotic usage of transactions as a determinant of Enneagram personality was denounced and changed. Essentially, everything boiled down to the psychiatric approach. Well, because this approach is more or less synonymous to the disorder of humans and this is why many people reject it for a better approach – meanwhile only those within the field love to use it. Whenever you read a book relating to Enneagram that utilizes this kind of personality developed, adjust your attention to their terminologies only.

Helen Palmer

Helen Palmer is the sort of Enneagram that focuses on the overall narrative of prevalent teachings. Just like this book, this development is in learning the general idea as there is no particular niche given. On a closing note, this Enneagram developed here is based on the teachings and approaches it had from its inception. It is not to nullify that Enneagram is based on the nine human personalities in their social relations and reactions to things and people. Based on this general background, it is believed that the development of Enneagram is from the first developer.

Oscar Ichazo development of Enneagram personalities

The Oscar Ichazo development is an approach that was developed as a way to give the application of the nine personalities, through the use of varying schemata,ego, for example. Psychologists and other great developers of Enneagram have agreed, at least to some extent, that those enneagram personalities had been in man since childbirth. Noting that there were not many new insights found when they traced the origin of the Enneagram to inhuman sources. In fact, the only thing that was discovered was the naming, description, and teachings of the nine Enneagram personalities which have been believed to be an influence of different developers explained at the beginning of this chapter. The line of enneagram development is evolving, and the probability of having much more approaches in the future is very high.

Lastly, note that the development of Enneagram has followed several approaches; however, none has ruled out the context of birth in the perception of the concept by the developer. This is one of the reasons enneagram personalities have many misconceptions even from the onset. The approach given here is the underlying factor which proves that Enneagram is a model and also a system of nine human personalities, using the names mostly adopted and not the popularly known misconception because this book will give you a complete introduction to the Enneagram personalities.

This chapter should familiarize you with the knowledge of the different school of thoughts in regards to the Enneagram. Having a deep understanding of where the concept originated from would also go a long way in putting you through a straight path concerning this journey. This chapter will help broaden your horizon as regards this concept. Now, which Enneagram school do you fancy? Which do you find appealing? Once you lay this foundation, the rest will fall into place.

Chapter 6: Enneagram Test

Checking Enneagram is no longer like the classic Myers-Briggs Type Indicator (MBTI), take a look at what you have taken (or at least possibly heard) before. In short, an Enneagram helps you find the specific qualities that make up your personality type.

Certainly, none of these varieties of character quizzes is 100 percent accurate, although gaining a high grip on your personality traits (your strengths, weaknesses, instincts, likes, and dislikes) will leave you at work and in your May help to enhance relationships. public life.

According to the Enneagram Institute, there are 9 Enneagram types and "it is common to find little of yourself in all nine types, although one of them must stand as being closest to oneself." The one who stands out. "Your basic personality type."

So what are the nine types?

Reformer - rational and idealistic type

Helper - Care and Reciprocal Type

Achiever (sometimes known as a motivator) - success-oriented and practical type

Creative (sometimes referred to as individualist) - sensitive and withdrawn type

Investigator (sometimes referred to as Thinker) - Excessive and brain type

Faithful (sometimes referred to as Skeptic) - dedicated and security-oriented type

Enthusiastic (sometimes referred to as generalist) - extroverted and spontaneous type

Challenger (sometimes referred to as Leader) - powerful and effective type

The Peacemaker - Easy and self-styled

One can also have a feather type. According to Electric Energies, "usually one has a type of symptoms that are adjacent to one's personality, which is extra outstanding - it's called a wing." "So whatever a type 5 is, it would likely have 4 wings or 6 wings. It could also be abbreviated to '5w4' and '5w6'. If one doesn't have an effective wing, it said It is known that the wings are balanced. "

There are a lot of Enneagram tests on the internet that promise to tell you your character type. So how can you understand which are valid and which ones are just a bunch of hocus?

Well, I did the legwork for you out of which 5 are in the most frequently viewed antennogram exams. Here's how well they worked for me in order from best to worst.

Personality Check Test

My results from this test: Mostly type 1 and type four two (equally), observed through type eight and then immediately observed through type 2, type 3 and type 7. It is a multiple-choice quiz with 36 questions that took me about five minutes to complete. This was meant to be a fast and easy task as an option, although some questions were awkwardly worded. The result of this check was not merely to indicate that I am a Type 2 (Helper), on the contrary, everyone keeps an eye on this list. Rather, it suggests that I am first and foremost, type 1 and type 4 (a reformist and artist, which means that I am an equal constituent rationalist and sensitive, which is probably the opposite of the truth…). Then I am a Type 8 (a Challenger), followed by Type 2 (Helper), Type Three (Achiever) and Type 7 (The Ampere).

If I am honest, there are many types here to understand. Of course, I can relate to all these types - all of us! But I no longer trust the accuracy that on a scale of 1-20, I scored 20 in two variants, 19 in one type and one 18 in three types. They are all in a very high type of ranking, which makes me query how well I bought it. I, of course, question the truth that, out of the five exams on this list, it is not the only one to have Type 2 (Helper).

Eclectic Energies Classic Enneagram Test

My results from this exam: Considering mostly a type 2 but, 2w3

I loved taking this exam, which consisted of 14 pages of 126 multiple choice questions, and I think the results are an alternative accurate. I feel that I am of the supportive type and I have a strong will to think of myself as a successful career-oriented.

That said, what I did not like about this test is the lack of context on the results page. The results clearly suggest that I seem to be "2w3" without any rationalization as to what exactly that says about me. For a test for so long, I would have expected a bit more detail by stopping it.

Composite Enneagram Test

My results from this exam: Mostly type 2 and type 4, followed by type 7

This test gives a list of symptoms for each anagram type. All you have to do is rate each attribute based on how well it is or will not suit you. It took me about 10 minutes before I finally demonstrated my result: more often than not Type 2, Helper, and Type 4, cautiously through an individualist, Type 7, enthusiast. These results are true and correct, aligning with the results I have obtained from other tests. I also appreciated how the questions in this check were put together across topics, so I felt that even if I knew how to give satisfactory answers.

However, again, I was not much aware that there was no explanation on the type - especially after so many questions. I have not been able to answer exactly how many questions, because the questions were not counted.

Fast Enneagram Test

My results from this exam: Top three types: type 2, type 6 and type 4

By the time I took the test, a whopping 2,464,348 humans had already taken it, making it an optional popular Enneagram test on the Internet. There are 36 questions in this one which you can complete in just 5 minutes. You just have to answer which of the two statements in each is the most difficult for most of your life. Then it takes exactly one minute for your effects to appear. Khan instead proved to be accurate.

The additional priority I gave about this test is that I now directed not only my own kind but also my top three types (again, Helper, The Loyalist and the Individualist), all of which resonated with me. Occur. It gave me broken explanations of each kind, so that I could investigate more about them - how to be with me, how to deal with me in intimate relationships, I like being that kind and hard to be. type. These are seriously beneficial figures when it comes to building my personality (and my needs, strengths, and weaknesses) into better relationships with others. And, to be fair, the whole thing written in this area was at some point.

What I did not like as a big thing about this test, he said, is the nature of question two - I often found it quite difficult to choose between two options. For some of them, I made an uncertain decision. Likewise, while learning about my pinnacle I was interested in three ways, yet I preferred to be given wings in a most important way so that it could be fully tapered.

Riso-Hudson Enneagram Type Indicator (RHETI) (Sample)

My impression from this test: Type 2 and Type 7 (equally)

I took the pattern RHETI exam, which is only 38 questions and takes about five to 10 minutes to complete on average. However, the full test, for $ 10 at the Enneagram Institute, definitely has 144 questions. Either, you can ignore questions that you don't practice, but you should not avoid questions because they are challenging to answer. I did my best to answer each one, answering which of the two completes every pleasant statement.

The draw to see is that you have to pay for the whole thing. Otherwise, I would argue that it is the most accurate one I have taken.

Chapter 7: Life Is Full Of Cyclical Temporal Traps

Now the time has come to think about the time and its way of arriving in cycles of events that are repeated and that we must be able to manage. time understood as personal, experiential time; history as a life story, events and teachings drawn from everyday life, behaviors borrowed from others, learned and reinterpreted in the light of their own canons, their education, their morals and their social sentiment. History of life, therefore, but with the clear I intend to reveal those "courses and appeals" that mark the moments; those gestures, those situations, those emotions that we often find ourselves emphasizing with the exclamation "Here, it happened again!". Life traps "or lifetraps, real ways of thinking, feeling, acting and relating that have been formed in fundamental moments of development and that over time have been structured into real traps. People often do not recognize them simply by identifying them with "destiny", thus surrendering to the possibility of changing their lives and subverting the patterns that determine them. However, some may recognize the dysfunction of the cage and choose to avoid the "active trigger" situation, or they tend to overcompensate with behaviors that are clearly opposed to those that actually belong to the scheme. What nevertheless appears clear, however, is that these cages do not allow for satisfactory and happy social relations because the people who are imprisoned do not really know either themselves or others. The schemes, in fact, are formed on the occasion of early experiences when the needs of the child have not been adequately interpreted by the caregiver, or by the figure of occurrence. The child has thus had to play force to hide his true Self and its emotional world, in favor of one more acceptable to the other which thus guarantees him closeness and care. It is therefore a matter of early maladaptive patterns, that is organizations of the experience according to distorted relational, behavioral, cognitive and affective patterns and fruit of the "sick" encounter between the child's temperament and his experiences with the caregiver.

We therefore understood how these patterns are formed, but what causes them to continue to operate? What keeps them active?

Since these traps are a way of reading and living the others and the world, in a pervasive and stable way, over time they are the most reliable compass for orienting oneself in relationships and with oneself. It is self-evident that this is a known, familiar and therefore "comfortable" and reassuring solution for the person when he finds himself answering questions such as "How are the others?" "What do I want?" does it move in the world? ". The trap thus becomes part of itself, a part that blends with its own Self and that clearly tells us who we are, who the others are and how we move around the world and, the most devastating thing is that, precisely because of the their "presumed truthfulness", we cling desperately, even paying the high price of pain.

So what are these traps?

Abandonment: we are convinced that we lose the people we love (by death or because we leave each other) and to be alone "Please don't leave me!"

Distrust and abuse: the abused person (abuse means any violation of personal, mental and physical boundaries) is constantly on guard. "I do not trust you!"

Emotional deprivation: the person experiences a real affective desert: loneliness and detachment, combined with a sense of emptiness and frustration of their own needs. "I will never have the love I need"

Social exclusion: one feels alone, isolated, excluded, unwanted and different with a consequent high state of anxiety.

Dependency: one has the feeling of not being able to do it alone, of not knowing how to look after oneself, therefore one needs constantly the help of others.

Vulnerability: you feel vulnerable, anything can happen at any time and you do not have the resources to face the situation with a consequent peak of anxiety.

Inadequacy: we feel something wrong inside, we don't feel adequate or worthy of love and we do everything to keep this hidden, with relative shame when instead this belief emerges. "I am not worth anything!"

Bankruptcy: we are considered to be bankrupt compared to others and, if good results are achieved, we feel like impostors, we think we do not deserve it.

Submission: one feels dominated by those around us; welcomes the other and is satisfied unconditionally. Passivity becomes a tool to get back a good self-image.

Strict standards: we must always do more and do better. One must be the best in everything one does, without ever stopping, without ever relaxing, with its anxious state that emerges if these standards have not been reached.

Claim: the others "owe" you respect, love, closeness and if this does not occur, you feel anger because you consider yourself a victim and feel frustrated.

Once the trap and its recursion have been identified in particular situations or with specific types of people, all that remains is to act and subvert the scheme.

Such as? Referring to small tips, useful for pursuing the path of personal fulfillment:

we awaken our "real" part which has been buried by years of submission, neglect, impositions, etc.; we listen to what he needs

we express our needs and realize our desires: very often we did not do this because we could not or did not think we deserved it; now instead dedicate yourself some time and above all think about deserving it

begin to enter into the perspective of possible change; if we want we can change, even if this will involve enormous effort

we become aware of our traps and try to implement a change with an intent that is constant over time. Obviously this implies leaving the known and the familiar to explore unknown personal and relational territories, but if we do not throw ourselves "in the fray" the change cannot take place by itself. Support our help

We begin to deal with situations and conditions that hurt us: it would be easier to implement those patterns that have anesthetized us for years, but if we really want to live with a new skin, we should not use shortcuts, but rather "try"; just so we will discover what we really are and want

Let's create a personal vision, or what we want and who we want to be. Ask yourself what really makes you happy, what makes you unique, what you really enjoy doing and above all consider yourself the only judge of yourself. Only you know what is good and what is detrimental to your person and, of course, respecting the rights of others, you begin to cultivate a healthy selfishness that allows you to speak in first person without feeling guilty or afraid of being judged.

Can the Enneagram help us achieve the one true purpose of everyone, that is, live happily?

If we exclude the mystical and esoteric uses, where this methodology of study of the personality has often found application, we will discover an effective system to understand who we are, how we relate to others and how to overcome our limits, in order to be happy.

Before understanding how to use this methodological approach to the study of personality, it is worth understanding why we should waste time informing ourselves about it. We have seen that the Enneagram substantially "classifies" people, consequently, if we know well the characteristics of each type, we can first of all understand ourselves, and secondly better understand others; since every enneatype brings strengths and weaknesses, being able to frame who we face, gives us the possibility to know him better, to know about things he has not told us (and maybe he doesn't want to tell us) and therefore to relate in as harmonious as possible.

At the same time we will discover how we are really made, that is what our weaknesses and abilities are, and therefore where we have to work to become better individuals and what to focus on to achieve the results we want.

It goes without saying that, knowing ourselves better and others, we will be able to weave better, deeper and more sincere relationships, in order to live better, because, I am profoundly convinced of it, true happiness in life is achieved by spending all of it the energies in the relationship with others, and giving very little importance to work and money.

The study of the Enneagram, however, has an even more interesting purpose than to improve oneself in relation to oneself and to others; the deepest secret is to use it to overcome one's limitations and obtain a truer and more complete world view. Most of our behaviors derive from well-established habits, patterns that we tend to repeat, for an unconscious fear of changing the status quo, breaking the balance in which we live and running into problems that we don't want. In reality this fear (we have talked about it at length) is unjustified and prevents people from changing, solving their problems, turning around the situation in which we find ourselves and emancipating ourselves.

The Enneagram helps us in this, to see things from a new point of view, through the correct interpretation of our behavior and that of others; in a sense it can be considered as a window on a new world.

At this point we try to understand how to exploit this powerful tool to "live better"; Let's take a look at the graphic representation of the Enneagram, a sort of nine-pointed star, enclosed within a circle.

Chapter 8: Enneagram Type 1

In this section, you will see eight good qualities, eight stressors, and eight stress behaviors of Enneagram Type 1.

Mark with a tick which ones apply to you.

Do not overthink; answer honestly and accurately. The more accurately you can answer, the easier it will be to find your type.

GOOD QUALITIES

Enneagram Type 1s are good people, both internally and externally. And something or someone is good if it is what it is and it does what it is supposed to do. 1s have a strong inner sense of knowing what right and wrong is. They are motivated not just to do good, but be good, and are motivated to live their lives according to a higher good or higher vision.

They value excellence and they make quality control experts. They have high standards and can automatically notice what needs improving. They are also generally organized people. They are tidy and they often have a system for their life. They like having a place for everything and everything in its place.

1s are hardworking and they work hard to make an honest living. They see possibilities in people and situations and they push to make their internal vision a reality. Their homes are often neat and tidy, and they work tirelessly in their jobs and roles. They are also generally punctual people, as it's just not good to be late and has other people wait for you.

1s are meticulous and they take care of their work. Whether it is just trimming a hedge, something just has to have the right look or the right feel. Enneagram type 1 is among the body types so there is an internal body sensation that tells them that things are just right. They pay attention to detail, are efficient and practical, as well as being idealistic and having high standards.

1s continually advance towards their ideal and they know what perfection feels like. They are geared towards progress and moving forward, and have a passion for doing things well and carrying them out to the best of their ability. They want to perfect every ability they have been given. They dedicate a lot of time and energy to perfecting their craft for you can always tweak something, and refine it to make it better.

1s create order. They are often active in the social arena and making social reforms. They have strong principles, they know what to do and they will teach you what to do. They can bring order out of chaos, for example getting kids to line up in a single file as they leave a school bus.

1s are educators and they hold high standards for themselves and others. They are mature and responsible, strict with others, but most strict with themselves. They feel compelled to interact and instruct others on the best way to accomplish things so that they reach their potential too. Their high standard applies to themselves, their kids, their spouse or friends, or even members of the public.

There often is zealousness to 1s, they have a strong inner conviction and they engage on a mission in making the world a better place. They are activists and can help introduce the rule of law, and religion to places where there are none so that the human spirit can shine through and make a difference.

STRESSORS

1s are overburdened by needing to adhere to their high internal standards and personal responsibility. They are part of the body type or anger type. The body is their center of intelligence and being respected and worthy is most important to them. 1s believe if they are not good, or right enough they will not be loved. Their body is their center of intelligence and tells them what is right and wrong.

They are the most emotionally contained of the 3 anger types. And when the world of a 1 is not as it should be, here are some of the things that could happen and some of the thoughts and beliefs that can pop into the mind of a 1 and cause them stress:

"I'm not a good person."

"It's all in the wrong order"

"I must keep working hard and improving things"

"I have to be so responsible"

"It's not perfect"

"This situation is chaotic"

"It's meant to be done another way"

"There's so much evil in the world"

ENNEAGRAM TYPE 1 STRESS BEHAVIORS

Here are some of the Stress behaviors that 1s will exhibit under stress. Mark with a tick which one applies to you.

1s become self-righteous and judgmental. They depend on upholding high standards of excellence and morality higher than everyone else's. They come to value being good and right above all other values, and judge other people's approach as wrong and flawed when they don't live up to their high ideals.

1s become highly critical of themselves and that can easily spill out onto others. They often have a checklist of criteria of what they are looking for in work and in people, and with a straightforward, direct, and honest approach they will find fault in what you think, do, and in how you behave. They appear 'better than' and constantly point out errors and how to do things differently.

1s strive in on the ideal and examine things through a magnifying glass. The harder they try, the more frustrated they become, and they may become compulsive and insistent that things are done a certain way. The ideal begins to overshadow their performance and the satisfaction they take in their work.

1s can become addicted to perfection. Everything can be improved upon or made better. This can make 1s easily dissatisfied and irritated that others question their way of doing things. They are also concerned with external order and see others as making an insufficient effort.

1s know they are right and they will speak authoritatively. They can become patronizing and condescending, giving numerous reasons to show they are right, and debate with others about any number of things. They want to make sure others get their point, and insistent on their position, looking down on the position of others. At which point other people lose patience, and become resistant.

1s are emotionally contained types, and they rarely share their emotions with others. But the more they get caught up in their perfection, the more tense and anxious they become. This manifests in a tense jaw and teeth clenched. They become overly serious. "There is only so much time in a day and I need it all to accomplish my mission."

1s must be scrupulous and self-controlled and they can become rigid and uptight. There is little time for lightness, and relaxing, and play must be constantly earned. "Why do I have to work overtime to make up for the laziness and irresponsibility of others?" They make themselves the sole judge on who is right or wrong, and their viewpoints can become very narrow.

Because of their sense of fairness and responsibility, If a 1 sees the other person as doing something wrong, then they should experience the consequences. But 1s are not in touch with their own anger, as being angry is also wrong. As a result, they have trouble releasing and forgiving and can become smoldering and resentful.

TEST RESULT

Here's how you interpret your Enneagram Test Results.

Scoring (one point for each tick):

Good qualities: 0 – 8

Stressors: 0 -8 (divide by 2)

Stress behaviors: 0 - 8

Divide your stressors score by 2, and add to your good qualities and stress behaviors scores for a total of 0 - 20.

A result of **12 or more** means you identify strongly with the Enneagram Type 1. It could either be your core type (1), your wing (2,9), or you could be connected to the type by a line (4,7).

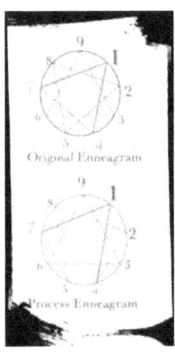

Chapter 9: Emotional Intelligence

The inner aspect of ourselves deals directly with our emotional psychology—it is the feeling and thought epicenter of every person. Some people worry a lot; others take things more in stride. Some are quick to anger, while others have a higher level of tolerance. There are many different theories out there on the psychology of self—many of which have differing opinions. Some people view understanding the self as very important, while others preferred to direct their intellectual energy elsewhere. David Hume dismissed self as nothing but "a bundle of perceptions." Others have agreed with his attitude, possibly because of the very emotional reality the concept of inner aspects present. Whatever we choose to believe about the emotional side of ourselves, one fact remains—emotions are a part of us whether we like it or not, and improving our emotional intelligence is a healthy approach.

Emotional intelligence (or "EQ") is one way of saying you not only understand your emotions, but you can handle them as well. Once we finally understand why we experience different feelings, emotional intelligence shows us what to do with them. It's the process of managing and appropriately expressing our emotions and the emotions of others.

The Hay group published an emotional intelligence model called the Emotional Competence Inventory. It identifies four essential aspects of emotional intelligence: Social awareness, relationship management, self-management, and self-awareness.

We've already discussed self-awareness in part in the previous chapter (accurately recognizing and analyzing your own emotions without letting them control you). Self-management is the ability to exert control over your own emotions. It identifies how we respond to different the events or stressors we encounter in our daily lives; whether we "react" or "respond." Are we quick to retaliate to the things or people that make us angry? Do we feel remorse or chagrin after specific reactions? Or do we take our time and control our reactions before we respond? Do we think about potential repercussions if we react irrationally? Reaction indicates an instinctual, reflexive response without much thought behind it. A response, on the other hand, shows that more reflection and thought has gone into the emotional outcome.

Relationship management is, of course, how we manage the emotions we encounter with other people. This can be especially helpful in the workplace. A large group of people will represent a variety of personalities. Some will get along better than others. An individual with good emotional intelligence will be able to mediate and resolve conflict much more quickly. Anyone can assist in resolving conflict; this does not just apply to those in leadership positions.

Social awareness relies much on empathy. Some are naturally more prone to empathize with what others are feeling, but anyone in search of a more in-depth emotional intelligence can learn to empathize. It helps us identify the strengths and weakness in a group making it easier to establish the "temperature" of any sensitive environment. An individual with a good grasp on social awareness will be better able to problem-solve and even take responsibility for mistakes rather than projecting on others.

Another psychologist by the name of Daniel Goleman created his own list of characteristics of people with high emotional intelligence. Self-awareness was also on his list, along with empathy, motivation, social skills, and self-regulation.

Empathy is the ability to understand and relate to another's feelings and emotions. It is what allows us to honestly evaluate a person's reactions before just jumping to conclusions. This also helps with conflict resolution and is a valuable trait to develop no matter our position or personality type.

A person with high emotional intelligence tends to have the motivation to set aside instant gratification to produce positive long-term results. They will also be willing to accept and overcome challenges and are usually highly effective in the tasks they take on.

Social skills are another factor of a person with high emotional intelligence. These skills help in a group or team setting. They can attribute success to the team as a whole without the need to claim it for themselves. A person with excellent social skills will be able to help others grow and develop. They are not afraid to let others show their skills and abilities. Building healthy relationships comes more easily, and good social skills also help improve communication.

Self-regulation has a reasonably obvious definition. It is the ability to maintain control over emotions, actions, and impulses. It helps keep negative emotions like jealousy or anger at bay to avoid acting before thinking through the situation and potential consequences.

Emotional Intelligence and Enneagram

We now know what emotional intelligence is. Now, we can use the Enneagram personalities to enhance our EQ.

Type 1 (Reformer): Reformers are excellent at motivating themselves and others. Emotionally, they are quick to anger and frustration and lack empathy. Ones can improve their EQ by learning to consider others' feelings and balancing their decisions and actions with more compassion.

Type 2 (Helper): Helpers are already very empathetic, and they live to help other people. Their tendency to ignore their own emotional needs is a familiar blind spot. They can improve their EQ by taking a step back and learning to allow time for them to address their individual emotional needs.

Type 3 (Achiever): Achievers are not necessarily empathetic, but they have the unique ability to adapt to a variety of emotional environments. They are similar to Twos in that they can get lost in others' emotions and lose sight of their own. Achievers tend to put emotions on the back burner to get their jobs done. To improve their EQ, Threes can change the way they consider feelings and include them to complete their tasks.

Type 4 (Individualist): Individualists are very attuned to their emotions. Because of this, they risk becoming a little too involved in their emotional state and ignore others. Learning to invest time in the opinion of another person consciously is one way that Fours can improve their EQ.

Type 5 (Investigator): Investigators are laid back and unprejudiced, but they can also be too disconnected emotionally from other people. They can improve their EQ by opening up to others in their relationships.

Type 6 (Loyalist): Loyalists come across as likable and naturally draw people to themselves but can come across as pessimists. To improve their EQ, Sixes can make an effort to encourage and build up rather than finding ways that things could go wrong.

Type 7 (Enthusiast): Enthusiasts are very positive people. They like to keep things exciting and usually tend to make that a priority. Sevens dislike challenging situations; they can improve their EQ by learning to embrace challenges and see difficult tasks through to the end.

Type 8 (Challenger): Challengers value honesty, and they are very transparent.

They tend to have intense emotions and are not always aware of how intensely they come across. They can improve their EQ by softening their emotional responses to others and being more generous and kind.

Type 9 (Peacemaker): Peacemakers strive to create harmony in any situation. They want people to feel comfortable in their surroundings, but they tend to ignore their own needs for the sake of others. Nines can improve their EQ by learning to acknowledge and voice their individual needs and emotions to avoid getting drained.

Chapter Conclusion

Emotions can be intimidating. As we can see by now, some personalities are better at processing them than others. Emotional intelligence is just as relevant as any other aspect of personal understanding and growth. There are many different ideas and methods available for learning about emotional intelligence. There are also many ways to improve it. Using the Enneagram model is helpful because you first discover the strengths and weaknesses of your personality. Once you have that information available, you have a good head start in the practical application of how to improve your emotional intelligence.

Chapter 10: The Power To Know Your True Identity

Numerous People think little of their intensity of really knowing yourself. On the off probability that you forget your real character, you won't ever be cheerful! Understanding your qualities and flaws, lands where you're normally better, along with your personality type, may provide you a gigantic little leeway over many people who believe they understand everything, except they are missing and generally despondent.

The Enneagram hasn't only stood the test of period; it's a field of advancement and inventiveness, always motivating new processes and practices for consciousness in otherworldliness, company, education, social networking, creating relations, brain study, instruction, child-rearing, sexuality, adjusting our own bodies and that is just the tip of this iceberg. Additionally, it's presently being educated in mind study courses in leading schools.

The stage when people first just recognize their respective Enneagram type and understand its own crucial differentiation, they often depict the encounter as like an otherworldly arousing. This can feel as if you have discovered a strategy of your soul -- each one of this causes you to one of a sort, in the same way, the similitude's that associate most of the people in ONENESS.

Also, the points of perspective that you obtain around what spurs other personality types can bring deep compassion, understanding, and arrangement for relational communication.

Winding up Throughout the Enneagram

Even though most of us have each of the nine kinds in ourselves, each one of us has our very own unique method to take care of the world that's seen prevalently through these kinds.

The main reason is that most of us grow up with a few body-mind-heart irregularities determined by our enneagram kind, which this lop-sidedness turns to the fundamental part of our apartment, sense of self-centred life. In the conclusion of the day, your conspicuous individual quality may concurrently become the most crucial impediment or debilitation for an entire blossoming for someone. The answer for each one of these nine types is to comprehend and relinquish this quality/constraint and open until the perpendicular world of Presence.

Obtaining Familiar with your personality is essential in this process of starting to shrewdness. Still, the aim of the enneagram is not to create an innovative character, for that is insufficient to convey us into the significant calibre of self-acknowledgment. This is where the vertical dimension becomes an integral element. The process of incorporation is not about what we "ought to" do-it is a process of intentionally relinquishing portions of our kind that square us. At the stage, once we quit clutching barriers, frames of mind, and anxieties, we encounter a pure unfurling and adapting as ordinary as the blooming of a blossom.

Relinquishing Yourself Through Spiritual Practices

Simultaneously, The Enneagram supports that on the off possibility that you use this extraordinary capability to encourage your own awareness of self, to strain your own incidence interestingly over the others, at the point your particular calibre can definitely cut you off from the real self, other folks, and your possibility of affecting the planet permanently. Distinguishing your Enneagram type, in there, also offers alerts about the possible drawbacks of your personality structure.

There, there is the dilemma of discovering gratification. Irrespective of how much accomplishment we've got about the horizontal plane, every single otherworldly convention says it'll not be adequate. We're seldom successful enough, renowned enough, or protected enough actually to be quite still. Otherworldly conventions are in understanding this disappointment is by strategy. Therefore, we search for our wholeness in that perpendicular, unending dimension.

Matters being what they are, how exactly do we retain the endowment of your personality yet purge its pretentiousness? How can we scan for pleasure beyond the level dimension? Profound customs suggest we as a whole have to perform otherworldly practices that will prepare to intentionally relinquish our apartment selves and rest from the vertical dimension.

Here Is a few increasingly supportive counsellors about methods: "The back kinds (4, 5's, and 9's) that can be remote from their own bodies may benefit incredibly from drifting manifestation, yoga, stretching, and in any case, jogging... For 3, 7's, and 8 -- the self-assured types -- linking with their spirits through loving graciousness manifestation and demonstrations of philanthropy" could be valuable. "1's, 2's and 6 -- the constant types -- likely won't consider going off to some quiet retreat or persuading a back rub to become otherworldly. To these internal voice-driven types, sitting thought seems something contrary to becoming obediently concerned about the welfare of the others.

Sort 8: The Leader

8 frequently are dumb or unfit. To process their enthused want and problems as identified by defencelessness, misery, and familiarity.

Breathing clinic: abstain from "fuelling up" with chest breathing so; instead, operate on breathing in your stomach to calm relax and down (take 10 moderate breaths once you feel you're blowing).

5 min web-based breathing action Chased by journaling regarding the day's events or recollections, focusing on vulnerabilities (e.g., anxieties equally as valuable things that occurred considering how these can be eliminated).

• An 8 wing 9 portrayed herself "stony-hearted," therefore that she chose two interrelated practices. She'd a Loving Kindness reflection, trailed by a representation where she watched her "restricted heart" opening to feelings and individuals.

An 8 wing 9 children felt He closed Himself to other people because he feared to become helpless. He chose to perform a 5-minute working motion, trailed by 10 minutes of documenting his feelings.

At the point, he'd audit what he wrote the next day. He believed that this training helped him to personality his own real sentiments and be ready to impart them to other folks, in the event he would so select.

An 8 wing 7 that regularly gets Sincerely fomented inside her relations opted to use a vast selection of expressions (cherishing thought, morning adulthood, breathing into remainder, and so forth), determined by the requirement at this time, to gather her up and open the centre to compassion towards other people.

Sort Eight:

Act with poise. You reveal real power if you subtract from saying your will with other people, in any event, once you could. Your real power lies in your capability to rouse and inspire people. You may accomplish more to validate the reliability and dedication of the others by demonstrating the importance of your own heart.

Sort 9:

The Peacemaker

I am considering that 9's demand inner stability, Numerous 9's are pulled into contemplation.

This may seem to be confusing. However, Numerous 9's have hidden outrage difficulties. Because 9's have to maintain stability, they often smother their aggravation. Using that which we have analysed about passionate reactivity, 9's need to determine how to comprehend and process their own indignation.

9's will generally like character Experiences, so mindful strolling along with other nature-based practices may be helpful.

Breathing clinic: Breath in the Torso to get vitality and keep away from midsection breathing to unwind, that is that the 9's regular condition and the manner that they "fall out" of existence.

These 9 wings 8 had to take a shot in her capability to get things to feel great in her own skin so that she did a 10-minute assurance contemplation. She felt exceptionally loose, grounded, spurred, and adventuresome through this training.

Sort Nine

Exercise frequently to prove to become mindful of your own body and feelings. Customary exercise is a solid sort of self-control and will enlarge awareness of your emotions as well as distinct senses. Exercise is also an adequate procedure to associate together and release hostility.

Sort 1: The Reformer

• An appreciation journal May Be Beneficial into the 1's who have a good fussbudget streak.

• 1's communicate a Terrific deal of Substantial stress, so extending or yoga activities can aid with this particular energy. "You may likewise wind up aware of methods you hold your body in particular stances, or how you can use more stress than ought to be expected when doing even simple undertakings. Anything out of a letter to driving a car ought to be possible with unwinding and attention or using snugness and obstruction" (119).

- Breathing clinic: The key for your 1 Is loosening up the gut, so go slow on the breath, extending this land and the rib limit. Give on the breath without keeping or pushing down. In the event you encounter tension, try to disperse the energy and feeling around the entire body, or do slow breathing to the gut.

- A 1 wing two had to take a shot Appreciation and forego her hair-splitting. Therefore, she'd an adoring benevolence symptom chased by correspondence writing to thank massive people throughout her entire life. Both practices assisted her to admit valuable things throughout her lifetime.

Sort One: Learn how to unwind. Put aside some attempt on your own, without tendency that everything is left up to you or what you do not reach will lead to tumult and fiasco. Tolerantly, the salvation of this planet does not rely upon just you, in spite of the fact you might here and there since it does.

Sort 2: The Helper

• You are doing a Loving Kindness Meditation That begins with all the considering oneself to work on acquiring your requirements addressed prior to managing the problems of others.

• This breathing manifestation encourages 2's to track their own energy -- coping with their own needs -- instead of focusing on other people.

• Breathing work Focusing on Yourself (not others), take a medium, complete breaths to your intestine, sending your energy to your feet and legs.

Sort 2: Attempt to prove to become aware of your thought processes when you opt to encourage someone. While achieving valuable things for folks is a splendid feature, when you do this on the grounds which you expect that another person should welcome you personally or accomplish something agreeable for you. Thus, you're setting yourself up for dissatisfaction.

Sort 3: The Achiever

• As mentioned previously, making and Pulverizing mandalas/fine artwork is a good practice to handle the fear of disappointment.

• Breathing clinic: Since 3 shop Up energy in the torso, the goal here is to inhale deeply from the gut and disperse the energy into the full body. Give until the breath onto a longer drawn out than normal breath outside, detecting the normal rhythms of your own body. This may open yourself to passionate attention.

Sort Three: Take breaks down. You may push yourself too, as some other folks to exhaustion along with your continuous quest for your own objectives. Aspiration and self-advancement are all fantastic features; nevertheless, temper them with rest intervals where you reconnect all of the more profoundly on your own.

Sort 4: The Individualist

- Since some 4 feels better than Others, 1 understudy chose to perform a contemplation followed by an appreciation journal. She believed it was really helpful.
- Another 4 decided to picture occasions When he revealed haughtiness in his words, deeds, as well as stances to empower him to observe how toward typifying prevalence. The aim was to boost his affectability to the propensity with the anticipation that viewing it's going to allow him to stay away from this particular frame of mind and run in the future.
- Breathing clinic: 4w3s must take Moderate, complete breaths and let go to the breath to release pressure, while 4w5s will need to work on breathing to the torso (and paunch) to create more energy. The purpose of the 4 is silent, lasting relaxing.

Sort Four: Don't consider everything literally, presuming that every remark is gone for you. What is more, irrespective of if one once in a while is, do not go over it on the mind? After all, a fundamental or antagonistic remark does not mirror every piece of pertinent information regarding you.

Sort 5: The Researcher

• Ever since 5 live such a Fantastic amount in Their heads, any type of instruction that puts them to the body -- cautious ingestion, focusing on eating routine, body curb contemplation, yoga -- is welcome.

• Breathing clinic: deep Midsection breathing will let you get grounded from the human body and in the time instead of always being in mind. Breathing into the torso will open your ardent focus to earn a compassionate institution with other individuals.

• A 5 wing 6 might have enjoyed to start His heart to others and let them come in his life. He'd make a loving generosity contemplation.

Sort Five: Learn to observe when your justification and estimating eliminate you in the instantaneousness of your adventure. Your emotional limitations are sometimes a fantastic blessing. Nevertheless, they could similarly be a trap when you use these to draw from contact with yourself as well as some other individuals. Stay connected with your physicality.

Sort 6: The Loyalist

• Together with uneasiness being a crucial component of this kind, 1 understudy who had been a 6 listed her worries and then dropped them as a practice to relinquish her stress. She believed it had been helpful.

• Breathing clinic: when you struggle, Flight, take a medium, complete breaths and extend the waist muscles, at the point discharge nevertheless much as might reasonably be anticipated to re-establish silence and reduce nervousness. Inhale in the chest once you want more energy.

Enable pleasurable senses to fabricate and love with lasting relaxation.

• A 6 wing 7 conflicts who struggles with Successive self-uncertainty and negative self-talk failed a continuous appreciation journal.

Sort Six: Many of your issues need to do with finding solid wellsprings of backing and direction outside yourself. Only your very own actual nature may provide you a deep sense of power and restrict on Earth, in light of how solitary the unconstrained understanding of your spirit can respond to each remarkable circumstance crisply.

Sort 7: The Enthusiast

• Ever since 7's vibe occasionally separated from their spirits, a contemplation that asks they start their hearts may be precisely what's required.

• Listed below are transcripts of people Since they're driven through a comprehension approach, which allowed them to move farther into their spirits.

- They are breathing clinic:7's exhaust Power "up and out" from their centre and to the gut so that they need to perform deep stomach breathing and sense feet on the floor to shield energy in their own middle.

Sort Seven: Happiness usually comes in a roundabout manner, as a consequence of offering something valuable. At the stage when folks are effectively drawn with their current involvement and possess their needs, they become optimistic without looking for gratification as their fundamental objective.

Chapter 11: Understanding Enneagram

Chances are you've already heard comments from numerous experts on the Enneagram. As you've already gathered, it is a symbol shrouded in mystical significance and the meaning and its different elements are not always clearly understood. This makes it difficult for some to embrace the idea; the lack of a direct explanation of the whole process often leaves some suspicious and wary, feeling that they may be entering a world of occultism.

For many, the occult is exactly what they think of when looking at the Enneagram symbol. Our minds automatically go there because it so closely resembles the pentagram which is directly connected to modern occultism. This makes many pull back out of fear that they are getting involved in something dangerously mysterious and dark. However, by examining the symbol exclusive of any preconceived notions and clearing your mind from those ideas people tend to automatically associate with it, we begin to see some similarities that we can find in other more acceptable beliefs of our society.

It's a natural part of who we are to want to know more about the origins of anything we get involved in, and while the explanation of the symbol itself can sometimes seem vague and obscure, we have been able to uncover enough to unlock the true meaning of the Enneagram symbol. It may take a little digging to find it behind the different elements, but it will be well worth your while to do so.

However, it is very important to point out that the Enneagram we use today has changed a bit from its original purpose. One of the best ways to decipher it is by starting with the human mind. It is a natural tendency for our human brains to view images and break them down into different categories. Nothing fancy, it's just what the human brain is designed for. Since Gurdjieff is considered to be the father of the modern Enneagram, many will automatically associate the modern Enneagram with his symbol. Gurdjieff's teachings leaned heavily on the metaphysical - a means of organizing natural principles and using them to explain how the universe actually works.

There were three basic principles of Gurdjieff's metaphysical theory, all utilizing the Enneagram symbol. The Law of Seven, Unity, and The Law of Three.

The Law of Seven: this law focused on the constant vibrations we all have around us. It is a little different from the Newtonian physics we have come to understand from modern science. Rather than what we've been taught - an object in motion stays in motion, the Law of Seven sees the world as a series of vibrations. According to this law, each object in motion must pass through seven separate stages before it comes to a stop. This means that the energy is not evenly spent but is instead lost at very specific points before it can receive an additional infusion of energy to continue along its path.

His theory was based on the seven note musical octave with the idea that in nature, once something is in motion, that motion cannot be sustained forever. No matter what it is, it must deviate or change at specific intervals. As you go through a musical scale, for example, as the energy vibrations increase or decrease, the consistent rate naturally changes at certain points. With music, the points have been identified as the mi/fa point, and the si/do point. So, in an octave of do re mi fa so la ti do, the intervals where vibrations change would be between the mi and the fa at one point, and the si and the do at another point.

Of course, there is a lot more to the theory of the Law of Seven that we won't go into here.

According to Gurdjieff, the energy that is spent in vibrations does not uniformly dissipate but instead is lost at very precise points where it can receive an extra impulse to keep it going along its path.

Unity: When you first look at the Enneagram symbol, your eyes will automatically recognize the circle first. This is the universal symbol of unity and infinity. It can also signify the oneness and eternal nature of a Supreme Being. To Gurdjieff, the circle represented two different forms of thinking. First, everything in the universe has a place; everything belongs with no exclusions. And secondly, the symbol was used to encourage a panoramic and more receptive awareness of the whole picture. This is done without judgment or labeling of anything as either good or bad. Anyone who can do this is able therefore to see the world in its true state and not be influenced by prejudices and personal preferences.

The Law of Three or the Triangle: This law represents the union of three fundamental things. First and foremost, the Supreme Being of the universe (God) determines its nature and structure. Secondly, its organizing principle, and finally - the power he has to pull it all together. All three of these elements are key to understanding Gurdjieff's teachings of the Law of Three.

It is clear that Gurdjieff's teachings were extremely complex and detailed but understanding just these basic facts is key to being able to grasp the true purpose of the symbol. As human beings, we have always been in a sort of quandary. On the one hand, we are always in search of our own individuality, but on the other hand, we have a powerful, inbred need to belong to something bigger than ourselves. While the western world leaned more towards seeing the individual to the point where nearly everything became disconnected, the eastern world strived for community and connectivity almost to the complete obliteration of the individual.

When you see the world with more importance placed on connections, the price you pay is a loss of human dignity which is sacrificed for the sake of the whole. On the other hand, when too much importance is placed on the individual, the cost is the infringement on the rights of others. Therefore, the ability to create a balance between the two is essential and having the Spiritual Being holding it all together is key. With a Supreme Being, both unity and diversity can have an equal part in our lives, and we learn to live for both ourselves and for others.

While the ancient history of this symbol may seem vague and elusive, our modern understanding can offer us an even clearer meaning. The more we learn about it, the more we can dispel the fears of its dark and mysterious origins. Today, the symbol is used primarily as a schematic on a number of different personalities.

While the symbol we use today is not exactly the same as the symbol that he used (it has been refined over the decades to be more applicable to the world's society of today), it has many practical applications once you begin to break it down. There are many different ideas as to how to use the symbol. With so many different personalities it is difficult at a glance to know where you actually fit on the personality spectrum. However, by the time you finish reading this book, you will have some very keen insight into the wisdom of the Enneagram so you can know exactly where you fit in the whole scheme of things.

Today's Enneagram

As we've already pointed out, the structure of the Enneagram is simply a circle with numbers and lines contained within it. Each of these numbers, circles, and lines can be analyzed and viewed from totally different aspects. In the basic Enneagram symbol, you'll first see a circle with numbers from one through nine around the perimeter in much the same way that the numbers go around a clock.

At first glance, the idea of a circle with numbered lines doesn't mean very much. At least, not until you begin to learn what each of these markings actually means. In the basic Enneagram symbol, the circle is a symbol of unity. The nine personality types are all equidistant from each other showing that they are all equal to one another. No single personality has more influence or power over any other. In essence, we all start on the same equal footing.

If you look closely, you will notice an inner triangle formed by connecting the points at the numbers three, six, and nine. This triangle represents a powerful and dynamic interaction of three different forces.

The Circle: You will see that there are nine different points spaced out around the circumference of the circle. We already understand that the circle is a representation of unity and the nine points are all equidistant from one another. This shows that each personality is equal but still connected to the others.

The Triangle: If you look closely, you will see an inner triangle that connects the three points at three, six, and nine. This represents the dynamic interaction of three very powerful forces. If you were to take two opposites, for example, the connecting force between the two would be some form of middle ground or a blend of each of the polar opposites. Here, three Enneagram Clusters are connected together by the triangle.

Hexad: If you were to look even closer, you would also see an irregular figure that connects all of the other six points. This part of the symbol represents the dynamic change we must all go through. As you will learn later, everyone has their own dominant personality, but it is not in control all the time. We are all constantly switching from one personality to another, each one represented by the Hexad, which connects them all together.

The Numbers: The nine numbers around the circumference represent the nine different personality types. Each type comes with its own seed of motivation that is responsible for triggering certain behaviors. While we all have a mixture of different personality types, we still have a primary or a stronger Enneagram type, which is responsible for our personal views on life, the actions we take, and how we respond to the world around us.

The Arrows: What you may not readily see in some Enneagram symbols are the arrows. However, if you see one with arrow tips at the ends of the lines, you'll notice that they follow a very exact structure that shows just how people shift personalities under varying circumstances.

When you are under stress, confident, or achieving a personal level of growth, your behaviors will automatically and instinctively shift from one personality to another within your Cluster. We will move along those connecting paths following the directions of the arrows.

Arrows moving backward represent your stress personality which is your automatic way of separating yourself from your usual behavior and protecting yourself from emotional damage. When some people face severe stress, they could switch to this stress point and remain there for days, weeks, months, and sometimes even years before they feel safe enough to return to their dominant personality.

On the other hand, forward pointing arrows travel a path to a more secure place that will permit you to perform safer behaviors. When you are at your security point, you are usually in familiar surroundings with people you can trust. When you are healthy, you might make a move to your Integration Point. This is where you blend together qualities that will create a delicate balance between confidence and structure. If you're looking to grow, it is important that you embrace these Security Points and follow those healthy behaviors applying them in your life.

By now, you've probably already begun to identify with a particular personality type. In fact, you've probably narrowed it down to several. If you're interested in pinpointing exactly which personality type you are, there are several resources you can find online that can help you. Some of them are free but those worth their salt will cost you a little bit of money to take the test. However, the benefits you can gain from this knowledge can be very valuable to you and can help you to improve your life in many different ways.

It is easy to see why so many people are intrigued by the Enneagram and what it can mean for them. It is a tool that gives you the ability to look at your own life and see it for what it really is. It provides the right frame for looking inside and identifying specific patterns that have been influencing your every decision since birth.

With this increased knowledge about yourself, you can feel empowered to venture off into different territories that reach outside of your personal comfort zone. As you do, your life's purpose will become clearer and your course in life, your destiny will unfold before you. Learning your Enneagram personality is just as much a spiritual journey as it is a psychological one, but if you take it with an open mind, it is possible for you to achieve greater intelligence about the human mind and discover your personal calling. However, it will require you to look deeper below the surface at what's inside for you to do so.

The Iceberg

Humans are highly complex creatures and are made up of many different elements. While we all have the same components, it is the unique combination of those elements that make us individuals. Your personality is made up of a delicate composite of several elements that reflect not just your inner feelings and experiences but also shows up in how you express yourself and interact with those around you. Each element has its own role to play in building up the personality that exists in you.

It has often been described as an iceberg. While the iceberg is massive in size, what you see above the surface of the water are simply those elements that you are consciously aware of. It is the part of our personality that we allow others to see. However, the vast majority of what makes us who we are is what lies beneath the surface, the part of us that either we are not aware of or the part that we will try desperately to hide from those in our lives.

These hidden elements are the very things that drive us to perform certain behaviors. To put it more simply, those hidden parts of our personality can be described as those things that we feel while those things that are visible to our naked eye could be viewed as the elements that inform us and we consciously react to. Together these all encourage our behavior and give us the motivation to do the things we do.

In order for the Enneagram to be most effective and beneficial for us, we must address what is both above and below the line. The combination is what provides us with the insight and the wisdom to make the changes we may feel we need to improve.

Chapter 12: Type Four - The Romantic

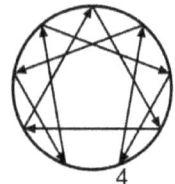

Dominant Traits

- **Temperamental**
- **Self-absorbed**
- **Expressive**
- Dramatic

General Behavior

Romantics are generally very sensitive individuals, especially on emotional matters. They can be moody when things do not go their way, and these mood swings can also be triggered by feelings or thoughts of someone or something. They tend to be honest about their feelings, yet at the same time, they are often concerned about their honesty, because it can make them vulnerable.

One of the best character traits of romantics is their creativity, which is evident in almost all spheres of their lives. They live for the big gestures in life, but even if they do something subtle, they do it in a creative way.

Romantics are expressive beings who make use of everything around them to show they are significant. Their value lies in their perception of their individual being. They need appreciation for who they are and the way they express themselves. This is the deepest form of understanding, so if you can connect with them at this level, it means you have been paying attention, and you recognize what matters to them.

One of their biggest pursuits in life is identity. It is very easy for a romantic to walk out of something - whether it is a relationship, a contract, an employment opportunity or even friendship - if they feel they are losing their identity within it. They feel strongly about who they are and, if they feel empty, a change of scenery can help them. They are always on a journey of discovery and rediscovery as is very easy for a romantic to sense that they don't belong somewhere, to which their go-to solution is to move to a place where they can be loved.

What motivates romantics to behave the way they do? In short, the desire to live their lives to the fullest. They crave a life in which they are not held back by inhibitions, whether personal, professional, or environmental. They love beauty and create it where they can so that their lives are filled with color.

The idea of romanticism can be confusing because many people assume it revolves around, attaching your life to someone or something. On the contrary, romantics are naturally individualist. They believe they are different from everyone else and don't wish to be held back by anyone.

They also tend to struggle with acceptance, thereby believing that it is impossible for other people around them to appreciate them the way they deserve to be appreciated. Many artists fit into this category, as have a predisposition to see themselves as special people solely because they possess unique skills or talents that set them apart from everyone else. At the same time, they struggle with an innate battle as they believe themselves to be flawed. They capitalize on this by engaging in activities that can overshadow their weaknesses and highlight the positive nature of their individuality.

Typical Action Patterns

In their attempt to express themselves and live the best of their individuality, romantics tend to seek answers in people they meet. If they feel there is something unique about someone that might fulfill their desire, they will stay. Even while trying to portray themselves as different from everyone else, they also try to establish deep connections with others.

Emotionally, romantics are very honest people. They are aware of their inhibitions and know what they are looking for, so they find it; they are bold and courageous about it. In general, they will choose a grand gesture to show you that you are the one they need.

Romantics struggle with insecurity. On the one hand, they are looking for love and for someone who will love them deeply and appreciate them as they are; on the other, they feel insecure about their weaknesses. They feel that deep down, no one can love them. They crave love, yet they feel they don't deserve to be loved. Because of this, they are insecure about their relationships, and if they are in one, they can guard it with jealousy. Romantics take it personally when someone disappoints them, especially people they hold dear. Disappointment can rock their lives to their core.

The most important step in the life of a romantic is to understand their personality. They need to identify who they are and what they want in life. Many of them know this already, but embracing the truth is different from identifying it. Many romantics try to use their close-knit relationships as a stepping stone to disprove to themselves and to everyone else that they are capable of being loved.

Their artistic persona makes them search for symbols from which they can derive value. This is good for them because unlike people, objects cannot disappoint them. This also spurs their artistry and allows their creativity to manifest in so many artistic ways. At times, it pushes them to form unhealthy attachments to people or things in life, as long as they meet a specific need.

Romantics are also very good storytellers. Most of their stories are expressed in a first-person perspective as they relate deeply with their tales, and hope their audience does the same too. By personifying their stories, they also create an opening for people to engage them and connect with them beyond superficial ties.

Typical Thinking Patterns

How does it feel too long for something that you know everyone, but you have? It can be painful and only gets worse when you know what you need, but you cannot find it. This is the life of a romantic. They are often envious of people around them who seem to have everything figured out, and these personal battles can overshadow their empathy and sow envy and jealousy. They cannot make sense of how easy and fast it is for other people to find their missing link, while their search continues on.

Many romantics suffer from emotional exhaustion yet they long for emotional fulfillment. There are a lot of things they need in life that they can't seem to find, and it bears down on them. They might seem happy when talking to you, but deep down, they are in pain. Because of what they seek, they resent pessimistic vibes. They believe there is something or someone out there that will complete them, and don't take kindly to anyone suggesting otherwise.

Romantics usually make decisions out of sentiment rather than facts. Facts to them are nothing but meaningless figures and information. However, beyond stating the obvious, they cannot reveal what they feel. Many of their decisions are based on what or how they feel about something or someone. Moving to a new town, for example, might not sound like a wise decision to many around them, but if it feels right and they feel a strong connection to the new town, they will ignore logic and move.

Nothing irks romantics like the idea of living an ordinary life. Ordinary is boring. There is no thrill or spontaneity, and an ordinary life means doing the same thing every day, meeting the same people and living life according to established rules and regulations. This is too inhibiting for romantics, and they usually find the fastest way out of such situations.

In their journey of self-discovery, romantics will come across people who do not understand them or what their lives are about. This becomes a problem because they take reactions like this personally. While romantics try to avoid pessimists, it takes a toll on them because they feel inadequate. Eventually, it can affect their self-esteem and make them feel unworthy.

Typical Feeling Patterns

Romantics are on a mission to find the missing link that can complete their lives. They are aware of what they lack, and they try to find it wherever they can. This explains why it is very easy for a romantic to move to a different town if they feel it is welcoming, and if the aura around that town satisfies a longing within them.

They feel strongly towards their ideas and feelings. Romantics generally connect with people based on what they feel, rather than what is factual, and they will trust their gut. If they don't feel a connection to you, they will walk away and seek satisfaction elsewhere. Because of their predisposition to feeling empty, they struggle with mood swings from time to time.

One of the standout traits of romantics is the way they challenge themselves to pursue self-discovery. They have an idea of who they are, and they try to find that missing spark. Romantics live life in the present. They focus on the opportunities that are available before them and try to find their place in society through them.

What sets them apart from everyone else is how they personify their struggles. They believe there is a reason for their suffering, and feel that at times, people don't get them because they are different.

When this takes a toll on them, it is easier to move on.

In order to find that missing link, they have to embrace their emotions to find what they lack, and what it feels like. This way, they will know when they find the genuine article. By exploring their emotions, romantics are capable of feeling deeply about people, activities, events, and anything else in their environment that means something to them.

People who feel deeply are usually the hardest hit when tragedy knocks on their doors and the happiest when the good times roll. Life with a romantic can be one hell of a carnival because most of them are free spirits. They live their lives one day at a time. However, they are also very serious about life and will take painful moments personally.

How to Improve Your Life

If there is one habit you need to drop, it is the tendency to postpone dealing with your feelings until a later time. The best time to confront your feelings is now. The next best time is right now. The fantasy world that you have created in your mind does not exist. Embrace the struggle and the pain in the same way in which you embrace the wins and the good times. Try to find productive projects that can engage your mind and keep you grounded with the world you live in.

Your feelings will often mislead you, so don't allow them too much room to control your life. While it is a good idea to try and understand your feelings, you should also realize that your heart and mind are constantly in conflict, each trying to outdo the other in influencing your decision-making. Don't ignore your feelings, but don't inflate their value in your choices either.

Be positive about life. This is the only way you can boost your confidence and self-esteem. Some of the decisions you need to make may be scary and push you out of your comfort zone but are bold as you make them. Commit to doing things that empower you and make a big difference in your life.

You might find solace in self-talk, but don't exceed your stay in your own head. Snap out of it, especially if you realize you are being too negative. Most of the imaginary conversations you have are unreal and only succeed in keeping you from experiencing real connections with the rest of the world.

Chapter 13: Protecting Yourself Against Unwanted Emotions

As an empath, you need to learn how to properly protect yourself against unwanted emotions. Hopefully, you have already been practicing shielding and grounding yourself based on what you learned previously, so you already have a general idea of how you can protect yourself. However, you may feel as though these methods are simply not enough as your energy may continue to feel exposed or vulnerable in certain situations. For that reason, you will need to address your protective abilities and find new ways to protect yourself against unwanted energetic experiences.

In this chapter, we are going to explore how you can protect yourself by creating your own shielding and grounding strategies to really help you experience protection against unwanted emotions and energies. This way, you can feel empowered to take full control over your energy and experiences as you proceed through life. In this chapter, you will learn about a few different shielding and grounding techniques and you will discover when each style should be used. Then, you will be supported in creating your own signature shielding and grounding practice that you will call on any time you need a strong anchor to protect you against your environment or those around you. You should also keep this book handy so that you can rely on other strategies taught here just in case you find that your signature protective strategy is not quite enough in certain situations.

Different Types of Shields

Empaths have access to quite a few different types of shields that they can rely on should they need to shield themselves in public or high energy places. In general, there are three shields you will likely want to rely on in addition to the white energy ball shield that you have already been practicing until now. These include a mirror shield, a spike shield, and a brick shield.

A mirror shield essentially requires you to first create your white ball energy shield around you and then mentally line the outside of your shield with mirrors that are pointing outward. This shield helps send energy back where it came from, which ensures that if anyone is trying to throw negative energy your way, it is sent right back to them through your mirror. This way, people such as narcissists who may be trying to harm you are unable to because their energy is being redirected back towards themselves.

A spike shield is one where you create your white energy ball shield around you and then imagine it drawing big spikes in towards you and big spikes out towards the universe. This blur the edges of your shield and helps you "mix" with the energy around you better without actually allowing it to penetrate directly into your personal energy field. This is a great shield to use when you are trying to blend in better, such as in busy public environments.

A brick shield is made the same way, starting with a white energy ball and then ending in you visualizing the entire exterior of your shield being covered in bricks. Imagine as though you are building a brick box around yourself, keeping you safe inside of it. These shields can be quite extreme so you should refrain from using them unless you are going to be in an energetically dangerous environment, such as one that involves a narcissist. That way, absolutely none of their energy penetrates into your space and you can remain protected and away from their destructive energetic field.

Methods for Grounding Yourself

Like with shielding, there are also many ways that you can ground yourself and keep yourself protected from the energies that may accidentally penetrate into your personal space. Sometimes, shields can have energy leaks or the pressure of trying to keep others' energy out can result in you having intense energy building up inside of your own energy field. This can become exhausting and can prevent you from experiencing a clear and comfortable energy field, thus weighing you down and increasing the burdensome feeling of being an empath.

When it comes to grounding, there are three practices that you can do in addition to visualizing roots extending from your tailbone or your feet and penetrating the earth below you. One involves the earth, and two involve water which, as you know, is fundamental in helping you navigate emotions effectively.

The one involving the earth is also known as "earthing" and requires you to walk around outside barefoot for a few minutes. Ideally, you should be doing so on the grass or in the dirt as these are believed to be the purest form of earth energy, connecting you deeply to the ground below. As you walk, the idea is that the earth draws unwanted energies out of your body through the soles of your feet and supports you in maintaining a clean energy field.

Another practice you can try is using Epsom salt baths to cleanse your energy in. Water itself is known for being cleansing, and salt is believed to ward off negative energies that may be lingering in your energy field and leaving you feeling weighted down and exhausted. By having an Epsom salt bath for at least 30 minutes, you can draw out unwanted negative emotions and leave yourself feeling light and refreshed.

If you do not prefer baths, you may prefer this third practice: cleansing showers. Cleansing showers can be used in combination with a visualization practice to help you cleanse yourself of unwanted negative energies. To do so, simply step into a warm shower and visualize the water washing away any negative energies or emotions that appear to be trapped in your energy field. If you would like, you can close your eyes and visualize the water rushing off of you as if it were turning black from negativity, and you can continue visualizing it until it turns clear. The visualization of the water turning clear is indicative that all of the negativity has been washed away and that you are now cleansed and grounded from unwanted energies and emotions.

Creating Your Unique Protection Formula

As with all forms of coping with being an empath and protecting yourself from external energies, you are going to want to generate your own unique protection formula to help you stay free of unwanted emotions. The best way to create your own formula is to start practicing the aforementioned shields and grounding techniques and to see what fits with you the best.

Below are the three steps that will help you in creating your own unique protection formula so that you can feel completely protected and grounded at all times.

Step 1: Practice All Methods

Practicing all of the protection shields and grounding practices outlined in this book is going to give you the best opportunity to try each shield on for size and get a feel for how it actually supports you in action. Each person will be drawn to unique strategies and will find that different practices work better for them or will fit better into their lifestyle, so do not be afraid to mix it up and see what fits best with you. You may wish to log your experiences in your empath journal so that you can recall how each shield and grounding strategy helped you and which one made you feel the best afterward. You should try using each method at least three times so that you can get a full feel for what the experience will be like.

Otherwise, you may find yourself not benefiting as much simply because it can take some time to properly put the method to work and grow from it.

Step 2: Assess Your Unique Circumstances

Once you have practiced with creating your own shields and grounding strategies, you want to make sure that you are creating a signature protection method that is going to fit most of your life experiences. So, if you find yourself consistently being drawn into busy places and feeling vulnerable and exposed, you may benefit most from a spike shield. If you are regularly exposed to narcissists or energy parasites, you may benefit most from a mirror shield with the occasional brick inlay. If you live nowhere near nature, you may benefit more from grounding showers or baths instead. Find practices that are going to fit your unique lifestyle and needs and start using them on a more consistent basis so that you are building on practices that actually serve you. Remember, the more you practice a technique, the quicker and more effective it will be because your brain and energy become familiar with this consistent practice. As a result, the minute you start, you will begin to experience relief from it because it is being used so frequently in your life. This is why having a "signature" style is so important: because consistency truly is the key to developing protection against unwanted energies and emotions.

Step 3: Personalize Based on Your Intuition

As you go along, you may feel intuitively called to customize your protective and grounding methods so that you can experience full freedom from unwanted energy or emotions. Perhaps, you are inspired to include a mirror on your spikes, or you want to both shower and use a soap bar with Himalayan pink salt in it. You may even find yourself being called to meditate and ground next to live plants or do something specific when you are protecting yourself that your intuition calls you towards. Lean into this calling and exercise it, as your intuition will best guide you in the direction that you need to go when it comes to protecting yourself. Always trust your intuition.

Your Quick Start Action Step: Protect and Ground

Your quick start action step today is to begin practicing just one of the shields listed in this chapter. In doing so, you are going to start developing a feel for what each shield feels like and how it serves you best. Focus on using the one that is most likely to help you the most based on your life circumstances and commit to using it at least three times over the next day or two when you feel that you need to. This way, you can start practicing creating that unique shield and putting it to work. If you find yourself being intuitively called to add a new step, personalize it in some way or another, or do something differently, do not be afraid to lean into that intuitive calling. This will only help you create an even stronger shield, so it is well worth your time and effort.

Chapter 14: Ennea-Type Five – "The Investigator"

Aliases: The Observer, The Scholar, The Thinker

The Intense, Cerebral type

Generally described as:

Perceptive / Secretive

Innovative / Isolated

At their best, Type Fives are described as:

Pioneers / Insightful

Visionaries / Inspiring

Motto: "I need to understand everything. The more I know, the safer and more likeable I'll be."

The Investigator in General

People who exhibit a Core Type Five have a strong desire to know as much as possible, and actively work to think deeply about concepts and possibilities. They place priority on curiosity and developing complex ideas and skills, and they value having something insightful and useful to contribute. Type Fives genuinely desire to be known for "having ideas" and being "independent thinkers."

They are dedicated to the topics they find interesting, which can become such single-minded focus that they lose connections with others. Investigators rarely explore popular or common topics, preferring instead to push the limits of knowledge at the boundaries, and because of their niche interests, can have difficulty finding others who share those interests.

When a Type Five person can fully engage and express themselves, they are inspiring, independent, and fascinating experts in their chosen set of topics. They enjoy sharing their unique, vast knowledge with anyone interested, but if no one is interested, they can become lost in their world of ideas. They make excellent sources of creative and innovative solutions, as it is naturally easy for them to apply knowledge and different perspective to new situations.

Sometimes, while Type Five people work to discover and develop ideas, they become protective of their privacy. Secretive, fearful of others misunderstanding and seeing them as inadequate, they hide their feelings, ideas, and thoughts. They can separate people in different areas of their lives, compartmentalizing their life to protect feelings and created identity. Investigators prefer to be seen as the "go-to" person on a topic and can detach from people or avoid situations that make them feel uncomfortable or incompetent.

When a Type Five person develops healthy relationships with others and feel respected for their expertise while learning from others' experiences, they feel fulfilled. For a Type Five, "a day without learning is like a day without sunshine." Their naturally inquisitive nature rewards them. They receive pleasure from not only "knowing things" but being able to expand on the ideas of others and contribute to the collective knowledge on a subject. Impressing others with ideas makes an Investigator feel worthwhile.

How Investigators See Themselves vs. How Others See Them

Investigators see themselves as genuinely invested in the progress of knowledge and the discovery of "truth", but they can also be detached, isolated, defensive, and judgmental. They think they are driven by a true desire to be seen as competent and capable, but actually, Investigators generally operate from deep insecurity and fear of being insufficient. They often seek validation from others, although they simultaneously reject this validation, which can become a self-defeating cycle where the Investigator feels trapped in a sense of inadequacy.

Investigators are invested in seeing themselves as innovative, sometimes despite the obsessions that result. While they desperately desire that others accept their ideas and discoveries, they may become insecure if those ideas are quickly and readily accepted.

Because Type Five people are so committed to exploring "big ideas," they can see practical, everyday problems as distractions from their larger mission. This can lead to Type Five people ignoring their basic needs and social obligations, or the emotional requirements of relationships. The irony is that the more an Investigator dedicates themselves to the study of a topic, the less they can care for their practical problems, which feeds their insecurities about being capable of functioning in the world.

While the Investigator Ennea-type can see themselves as the embodiment of progress – because, in their view, they always work to "better" humankind – they can come across as closed-off, focused on strange or irrelevant topics, eccentric, or out-of-touch with reality. The Investigator can see themselves as an instrument of innovation, but it may appear to others that they are actually disconnected from people and real-world problems of day-to-day life. While Type Fives may find fulfillment in collecting and demonstrating their knowledge, it can be frustrating to others when the ideas are too complex or narrowly focused to be practical.

The "Average" Investigator's Mental Health

When an Investigator is at an average level of mental health, they may feel deeply in-tune with interesting subjects, able to apply the information to new situations. They are curious and intense, which can make them narrow-mindedly focus on rare or niche topics. Sometimes argumentative, Investigators at this level are determined to show that they know what they're talking about and their knowledge is valuable.

When an Investigator feels better than average, they may be full of joy and enthusiastic to share their new knowledge, sometimes imposing or intruding on others. They come to decisions after long deliberation but act efficiently once they reach a decision. Healthy Investigators want everyone to appreciate the love of learning for itself, as well as practically apply knowledge in fun, creative ways. However, they may become fascinated by subjects that don't resonate with the people in their lives or their community.

Moving Toward Integration: Investigators At Their Best

When moving in their Direction of Integration (growth) and exhibiting their best qualities, Investigators become confident problem-solvers and decision-makers, focused on teaching and helping others, and are able to shed their defensive self-centeredness.

Basic Desire(s): To be capable, competent, dependable.

Basic Motivation(s): To "understand everything," to "collect" knowledge, to solve problems, and to be useful. They work hard to show their ideas as worthy and valuable.

Unique Gift(s): Knowledgeable, respectful, mental clarity, reliable, thoughtful.

Basic Goal: To arm themselves with knowledge ("know everything") in order to defend against change, uncertainty, or environmental threats.

When Investigator's Mental Health is Excellent

When at their best, Investigators are capable, competent, and perceptive. They become not only curious, but flexible in their perspective, able to see both the "big picture" and the "small details." Pushed to discover, driven to explore ideas and question established topics, they embody natural curiosity and pioneering spirit. Their high level of energy for collecting and harvesting knowledge, combined with their attention to detail, make them a formidable force in any area of expertise.

As Type Five people Disintegrate, they shift their focus and appreciation for mastery away from people "in front of them" and toward more "distant" people and ideas. They can withdraw, applying their mental edge to something inside themselves, sharpening their ideas until they feel they are "presentable" and "worthy" of being shown to others.

Moving Toward Disintegration: Investigators When Stressed

When moving in their Direction of Disintegration (stress), the normally inquisitive and focused Investigator regresses toward becoming idiosyncratic, disorganized, even frantic.

Basic Fear(s): Worthlessness, uselessness, incompetence.

Triggering Emotion(s): **Greed**

When Fixated: Become secretive, withdrawn, stingy.

What Type Five People Might Struggle With

Type Five people suffer from preoccupations and obsessions with impractical, esoteric, or unnecessary ideas. This can contribute to a sense of isolation, and although they are desperate to connect with others, their limited focus on intellectual connection can prevent them from seeing the importance of physical and emotional connections.

At times, Type Fives can become narcissistic, judgmental, intense, and even nihilistic. In order to establish themselves as "smarter" than others, they can become critical of other people's ideas, attitudes, and ignorance. A Type Five person might spend such immense amounts of time and energy in a specific topic that they ignore or disregard the importance of topics that resonate with others.

Type Fives tend to let their imaginations run wild and ignore the world's pressures as they escape into fantasy and idealism. Relentless pursuit of their own identity through knowledge can both make them feel safe and vulnerable at the same time. If they cannot be safe in their minds, they often cannot find safety in others, and so have difficulty trusting people, although they intensely wish to appear trustworthy and reliable.

When Investigator's Mental Health is Struggling

When fully disintegrated and under stress, Investigators become obsessed with their ideas and inner realities. They can withdraw fully, becoming reclusive and eccentric, and even engaging in self-harm or self-destructive behaviors. Fearful and self-absorbed, they reject relationships in favor of worlds they construct in their minds.

As Investigators decrease their stress and focus on their health, they become more attached to others and accepting of limitations in themselves and others. The healthier an Investigator's mindset, the more they can free themselves from their self-imposed restrictions and expectations and express their loving and compassionate nature.

Potential Addictive Struggles

Type Five people might struggle with poor hygiene and self-care habits, as they can neglect their health, nutrition, and physical needs when engaged in their passion. In some cases, extreme reclusive habits cause them to be hazardous to their own health.

Some Type Five people might struggle to addictions or dependencies on hallucinogens, alcohol, or prescription medications to escape anxiety related to the pressure to "know it all," or to expand their experience.

Overcoming Challenges of the Investigator Ennea-Type

It's important that the Investigator establish their own identity and cultivate an area of expertise, because if a Type Five cannot find value in their own intellect, they regress to a sense of purposelessness and meaninglessness in "everything." Rest, empathy, creative connection with their emotions, and the chance to present themselves as role models can help the Investigator stay balanced and at their best.

Being the Best Investigator

Harness the best aspects of your Investigator Ennea-type and diminish negative traits that emerge under stress. If you're an Investigator, or know someone who is, consider using the following techniques to help unlock and grow the best version of yourself.

Mind Your Mind

Type Five people need to be self-aware of their emotions and needs. They see possibilities but can become paralyzed by the need to make decisions, retreating into the world of their ideas for security. To maintain balance, an Investigator must recognize when they're ignoring or retreating from their physical and emotional needs, then push themselves to reach out to others for comfort. Investigators can have difficulty letting go of their "need to know," so learning to ask for help presents them with challenges. They must recognize that they can't know everything and that there are other things as important as knowledge.

Type Five people find joy in relaxation, reflection, and learning from perspectives that they aren't regularly exposed to. They may not cognitively enjoy, but will emotionally benefit from, being pulled out of their internal world to engage "in the now." They can also learn how to focus their involved decision-making process toward everyday tasks by learning to place priority on their needs and emotions.

Suggestions:

Meditate. Practice yoga. Build confidence by practicing making small, practical decisions and small, significant achievements. Use a daily to-do list to monitor emotions and activities that are focused on non-intellectual pursuits. Walk in nature. Read or write poetry. Draw. Paint. Dance.

Focus Nervous Energy

Type Five people naturally love to share what they learn, and they want others to be excited about learning. When they refine their skills to teach, they have huge impacts on those around them. The Investigator at their best finds joy in educating, instructing, and helping others to hone their own natural skills and love of knowledge.

Although an Investigator can become frustrated and impatient when their high levels of energy outmatch those of their students, learning to cultivate their patience and focus their nerves can help the Investigator be more productive, efficient, and compassionate.

Suggestions:

Converse with a trusted friend or colleague. Relax with video, board, or card games with others. Engage in group therapy. Mentor, volunteer, tutor, or lead a group. Engage in exercise – especially with a group. Practice learning physical and practical skills to see yourself as a learner while also directly connecting with people who are experts in non-intellectual areas.

There are simple things an Investigator can do to release their deep understanding of ideas and concepts into practical, useful ways for others, especially when they give themselves permission to be vulnerable.

Chapter 15: Enneagram Type 5 - The Observer

Triad: Type 5 is a variant of the core type of the Mind Triad, with Type 6 being the core type.

Core Belief: People and situations drain me of time and energy

With this core belief, the Fives' focus of attention is on whether demands will be made of their time and energy. This operates below the level of conscious awareness and underlies everything that they do.

Fives belong to the Mind Triad and are therefore comfortable in the realm of thoughts. As with all Mind types, safety and security are a concern for the Fives and their approach to dealing with this is what separates them from the type 6 and type 7.

Fives learn to isolate themselves from people, who could drain them of time and energy, and are comfortable in their own company. They are happy to watch and observe situations from afar rather than risk being in the situation itself. They like to have time to themselves to analyse what it means for them and to 'replay' them again in their mind. Fives are analytical and objective; they have the gift of being able to accumulate and master vast amounts of knowledge and concepts. They have the ability to put together seemingly unrelated pieces of data and come up with a connection/theory. The world of the Five is where many geniuses reside.

The ability to live in the mind to a high degree allows them to create great and complex worlds from their imaginations. As they tend to avoid people, Fives are generally reclusive and people around them don't know them well. The Five's home is his/her castle, where they can retreat behind the walls and feel safe. The walls could be the real walls of their residence, or they could equally be a wall of books / computers in their office. Living inside the realms of their mind most of the time, they rarely require social skills and so are perceived as awkward, 'geeky' people by the rest of society. Often they become social outcasts and are made fun of by people who don't understand them. Given their own time and space, not being rushed into anything, Fives will open up to people that they learn to trust. Those fortunate enough to be invited behind these walls will often find a sharp thinking, witty and sensitive person.

Seeking knowledge and avoiding people also can become the blind spot of the Five. They can develop an intellectual arrogance from their wealth of knowledge. They can withhold information from those who need it and appear scrooge like with their resources. At their weakest they can become stubborn and critical of others.

Examples of Fives (real and/or fictional)

Albert Einstein and Bill Gates

Filmmaker George Lucas

Authors Agatha Christie and JRR Tolkien

Robin Williams' character in the film One Hour Photo

Hannibal Lector in the film Silence of the Lambs

As the name suggests, this personality type watches the world go by from the safety of their ivory tower. They aim to achieve greater clarity and understanding of the world around them. They don't like confrontation or dissent so tend to take the third party view, refusing to get involved in any family squabbles.

They tend to make headstrong leaders as they are fully confident in their own abilities. They "know" that they will either have a deeper understanding of the subject matter already or else have the ability to learn it. Observers are happy to make decisions in the workplace as they believe in logical thinking but will pass the responsibility for emotional decisions i.e. those involved in a relationship to the other party.

The positive aspects of this personality type are their curiosity in people and the world around them, and this makes them willing to try new ideas. They have great courage and tend to be non judgmental of other human beings. They encourage others to develop their own independence as they are happy to delegate and trust others in their team.

The negative behavior with this personality type is, as with the other types, a distortion of their strengths. As they are analytical by nature, they believe that everyone is in control of their life so can be quite unsympathetic. They do not believe in fate so any misfortune you may suffer is down to your own incompetence.

Observers tend to be very bad at asking for help as they believe that they already know everything they need to know or have the ability to find out. This makes them very resourceful people but they can also be difficult for others to live with.

Conclusion

The Enneagram is probably one of the most open-ended of personality typing systems, and this is one of the best things about it. However, this does not mean that it uncovers all there is to know about human beings.

The core principle that lead to its development in the first place is that individuals are analyzable only up to a certain point. There are no simple tricks and explanations to how the human heart, mind, and spirit operates. We can only take the Enneagram as a starting point. The patterns it provides will help you take the first steps but you will have to keep going so you can find the profound truth about your true identity and your own place in this world.

This is just a reader's digest version – so much more to learn, and more importantly to implement in your life. Join the enneagram community and try to listen to Enneagram teachers to determine what resonates with you.

Finally, remember that the enneagram can only help us if we are completely honest with ourselves.

Thank you downloading this book. I hope you enjoy your journey.

www.ingramcontent.com/pod-product-compliance
Lightning Source LLC
Chambersburg PA
CBHW072013070526
44583CB00015B/1463